Margar[...]

28, Wes[...]

Edinburgh 9.

D0192569

THE PATTERN OF
ATONEMENT

THE PATTERN OF
ATONEMENT

H. A. HODGES
Professor of Philosophy
University of Reading

SCM PRESS LTD
56 BLOOMSBURY STREET
LONDON

First published 1955
Second impression May 1957

Printed in Great Britain by
Robert Cunningham and Sons Ltd.
Longbank Works, Alva

Contents

5

Preface

THIS BOOK is a revised version of a course of lectures which I was invited to give in Passion Week, 1953, at the *Schola Cancellarii* in Lincoln. It was thought that the lectures, intended in the first place for theological students, might be of interest to a wider public. The text which now appears has been extensively rewritten, but there is no change in the ideas expressed.

The treatment of the subject is not devotional, but expository and critical. In the first two lectures I have tried to build up a balanced picture of the economy of our salvation, drawing the evidence from the Bible and the liturgies of Christendom rather than from Atonement theories in the more technical sense. In the last three lectures I have analysed critically some of these more technical theories, including the controversy over justification by faith. It is hard to reach a conclusion about this momentous controversy without being led to say things which will appear to one side or the other to be unfair. I have tried to keep in mind what must always be the true aim of discussion in these matters – to discern the truth while at the same time understanding why the error is so passionately maintained. I shall be happy if those readers who think I have myself embraced the wrong conclusion are helped to understand from what sources my truth (which they think error) draws its enduring power.

H. A. H.

Reading
August 1954

I

The Five-Fold Problem

THE WORD 'atonement' is a native English coinage. As we all know, it was put together out of the two English words 'at one' and originally the verb 'to atone' meant bringing together, into a relation of friendship, two or more people between whom such a relation had not previously subsisted. There is nothing in the etymology of the word to suggest that these must be people who had once been friendly but had become estranged; but in actual speech the word has come always to be used with that implication. Hence to atone is to reconcile, and atonement is reconciliation.

At first one spoke of 'atoning' two or more people, i.e. reconciling them. 'Atonement' was the process of bringing together people who had been estranged. But estrangements do not take place without reason; where there is an estrangement there has been an offence, and where there has been an offence the estranged parties cannot be atoned unless the offence somehow has the sting taken out of it. Because of this it has become possible to speak 'of atoning for' the offence i.e. taking the sting out of it so that the parties can be reconciled. This is the process which is called in Hebrew 'covering' the offence, and the day which in Hebrew is *Yom Kippur*, the Day of Covering, is in English rightly named the Day of Atonement.

If the sting is to be taken out of an offence, it must be by something done for that purpose. And this action, the action which 'atones for' the offence, can also be called an 'atonement'.

Theologically, of course, the term 'atonement' applies to the reconciliation of God and man, and it can be used either as a name for the fact of reconciliation, or, more narrowly, as a name for that particular act on the part of the reconciler which makes the reconciliation possible by 'atoning for' the offence. In the first of these senses the Atonement is coextensive with the whole work of Christ. The whole of that work can be seen as a bridging of gulfs, a removal of estrangements, a restoration of unity. But in the narrower sense the Atonement means some particular part (the crucial part) of the work of Christ, that part without which the whole work of reconciliation would not be possible. It is not merely that Christ has reconciled man and God; He has done something to reconcile them. What is it that He has done which has this effect? This, in the precise sense, is the problem of the Atonement.

If one looks at the articles headed 'Atonement' in the theological encyclopaedias, one finds that they present a dreary prospect. They deal with the Atonement in the narrower sense, sometimes without troubling to indicate that there is a broader sense, and their manner of dealing with it is to give a list of 'theories' which have been put forward as descriptions and explanations of the Atonement. Some of these theories make a modern reader open his eyes, some of the terminology offends his ears, some of the material is so dead that one feels it must have been still-born. Everywhere one moves in an atmosphere of the driest theological speculation, whose relation to the actual Christian life is apt to appear tenuous.

Things seem to have got steadily worse since the end of the patristic period. Though the labour of thought has been continuous, and theories have multiplied, they have not become more convincing as time went on. After the Reformation, which made the Atonement the central issue in theological debate, a very difficult situation came about. In wide circles of Western Christendom the Atonement became identified with one particular theory of the Atonement. Men could no longer conceive that there might be other accounts of it and, the theory in question being one that offended against reason and justice, 'atonement' became in the end a word of bad odour. A vigorous folk-memory of this false theory is still part of the mythology which passes current as an account of Christianity among our non-Christian contemporaries. Within the Church in recent years the false theory has largely died, but has too often been succeeded by an embarrassed silence.

I once read somewhere that the Church is just beginning to escape from a liturgical ice-age of many centuries' duration. I would say that there has been an equally long-lasting soteriological ice-age, from which it is full time that we should escape. But there can be no escape so long as we attempt to discuss the Atonement in the narrow sense alone. We must recover a sense of the wider context to which that belongs. Only then shall we be free from the tyranny of the theories, their endless inconclusive debate with one another, and the blind revulsion against them all which is so natural a feeling and so perilous a guide. Only then shall we be able to do justice to them, and upon them, when we see the whole picture of which they pick out and isolate certain features. In these lectures accordingly I shall begin by trying to present that picture in a full and balanced way. I shall not begin with the theories, either by tracing their origins and their history or by setting them forth in the abstract and weighing them against one another. That is not the surest way to the truth; nor would one expect a philosopher to approach the subject in this way. I shall take for my subject the whole work of Christ as peace-maker and restorer; I shall try to describe that work as Scripture and experience present it to us; and when I analyse, it will be a philosopher's analysis, taking for its object ideas and standpoints rather than books and writers, and aiming at clarity for the sake of proportion. If we begin in this way, I think we shall find that the theories come into view at the proper time, and in a context in which they can be understood.

Christ is a peace-maker and a restorer. To whom, or to what, does He bring peace and restoration? In the first place, of course, to mankind. *Jesus hominum salvator.* The story of how man fell into mortal danger, and how he was delivered from this danger by Christ, is a vast and noble epic foreshadowed in many myths, dwarfing and at the same time illuminating the whole history of recorded time. We shall have to examine this story as Christian tradition presents it to us, while remembering that though it is centred on man it does not confine itself to him, but widens out to include the whole universe in space and time. For when man fell, nature too was in some way dragged down with him, and now waits, according to St. Paul, in travail and in dumb expectancy to find its own deliverance in his. With man's restoration nature is restored, with man's glorification nature is glorified, and the perfected Bride of Christ finds her home in a new heaven and a new earth. This is the full story of the saving work of Christ. This is the true Atonement. The whole mundane creation, made by God for God and temporarily alienated from its maker, is drawn back into union with Him.

In scrutinising this story we must have an eye especially to the imagery in which the Bible and Christian tradition have clothed it. For this imagery, indispensable though it is for a full expression of the truth, has also proved open to disastrous misinterpretation. The human imagination, here as elsewhere, assimilates the less familiar to the more familiar. We are familiar in human life with the phenomena of offence, estrangement and reconciliation; we know how these things work when human beings are involved, and we stupidly suppose that it is the same when one of the parties is God. So we impute to God our own attitudes, purposes and methods, and construct the theory of an atonement such as we ourselves, if we were in God's place, might contrive and approve. The result is a caricature of what God has actually done, as it always must be when we judge the things of God on the analogy of human experience instead of judging experience by the analogy of faith.

To understand a process of restoration we must understand what it is that has been lost or damaged. To understand a deliverance we must understand the nature of the trouble or danger from which someone is delivered. To understand the process of man's salvation, therefore, we must understand from what evil state or condition man needed to be saved. Man, we say, is a 'fallen' being. What is the reality behind this image of 'falling'? Everyone knows that the answer is 'sin', but what in turn is 'sin'?

The New Testament words which are used as names for it tell us something of its nature, though by no means all. There is *hamartia*, which, as we are all tired of hearing, means missing the mark. There is *parabasis*, transgression, i.e. stepping out of the right path. There is *paraptoma*, which means falling out of position as, for example, a stone in a building might do. Behind these three words a common idea is visible, the idea of the wrong place or the wrong way. Then there is *anomia*, lawlessness, *adikia*, injustice or unrighteousness, and *asebeia*, impiety. These three again convey a common idea of failing to do something which ought to be done, failing in obedience or respect. Both of these, *viz.* going wrong and failing in duty, are truly aspects of sin, and, as will appear, they relate especially to one aspect of our fall and of our salvation. But this is not the only aspect, nor the only important aspect, of the matter.

We see things in a fresh light if we look not at our catalogue of New Testament words, but at the conception of sin as disease and salvation as healing, which runs through the Old and New Testaments alike. It is in this light that we must interpret the miracles of healing reported in the gospels. They are not merely acts of mercy, performed for the relief of human suffering. They are the 'works of Messiah'; they are His credentials as Messiah. He offers them as such to the enquiring disciples of the Forerunner. In healing sicknesses of body and mind He displays in typical form the healing work which He is to perform also on soul and spirit, and an examination of the types of sickness with which He deals presents us with a list of attributes which throw light on the nature of sin. Sin is fever, weakening the patient; it is paralysis, rendering him incapable of movement; it is leprosy, progressively rotting the fibres of his being; it is blindness, dumbness, deafness, lameness, depriving him of the power to perform functions which belong to his nature; it is epilepsy, a sudden uncontrollable paroxysm, afflicting and at the same time endangering the patient. At its worst it is more even than this; it is demonic possession, and the healing has to take the form of an exorcism.

Elsewhere in the Bible we find yet another set of images which add to the picture. We find sin or its consequences described as darkness, or as captivity, or as exile, and finally as death. Salvation correspondingly is light to those who sit in darkness, the liberation of the captive, the return of the exile, the raising of the dead.

Such is the material that the Bible presents for an understanding of our necessity and of the work of the Saviour. But let us now try to distinguish and analyse and draw out what is implicit in these images. It may, I think, profitably be put under five heads; and these will make visible to us the five-fold problem of salvation.

I. THE BREACH OF PERSONAL RELATIONSHIPS

Man was made for fellowship with God. So much is implicit in the mere fact of his being made in the image of God. It is not only that like is drawn to like, but the nature of God is itself a social nature. Personality and society, which in human life fall apart, are one in the Blessed Trinity. So, if the image of God is to appear in human persons, it can do so fully only in so far as they are drawn into fellowship with one another and with Him.

It is perhaps legitimate to find some hint of this in the

creation story. 'God created man in His own image; in the image of God created He him; male and female created He them.' Not that we are here invited to think of God as bi-sexual, but that the distinction between the sexes demands their union and brings about the family, the primary cell from which all other human societies arise. And human societies are not exclusively human. The family, along with more complex and derivative forms such as the nation, the kingdom, the city, is presented in Scripture as a form of society in which God and man can share membership. The Church, we read, is the family of God, and He is the Father of the family, and from that fatherhood all fatherhood on earth takes its name.

The creation story goes on to give us a picture of the first (which is also the archetypal) family in the days before its de-generation. For this, of course, is the true meaning of Eden. It has often been supposed that the unfallen Adam and Eve must have been in possession of physical, psychical, and intel-lectual powers which have since been lost, and in itself the idea is wholly reasonable. (It does not mean that they were in actual possession of all the knowledge and skills which the exercise of those powers could in the course of time have obtained for them.) But we must be very clear in our minds that the glory of unfallen man did not consist in the possession of such powers. The biblical Adam and Eve are not a pair of culture-heroes; they are something quite different, *viz.* an archetype of man living in the Presence. They are the original human family, centred on God, living in intimate unity and understanding with themselves, with one another and with nature so long as they are in unity with God. Adam and Eve are made for one another, complementing one another, completing one ano-ther's nature as human beings; together they are given authority over the lower creation, together they are charged to be fruitful and multiply their own kind, but their prosperity, and power, and harmony with one another depend on their recognising a responsibility to God, and living in obedience to a wisdom greater than their own.

I have spoken of man's 'responsibility' before God. To be 'responsible' is to be 'answerable', i.e. liable to be called to answer for oneself, and the Bible always assumes that man's relation to God is a relation of this kind. There is true biblical theology in the saying that man has his being in the Word of God. The worth and dignity of man's nature lie in the capacity which he has for hearing and obeying that Word. True, there is a broader sense in which not man alone, but all created things can be said to be thus obedient. Wind and storm 'fulfil His Word', floods rise and fall at His command. But for winds and storms and floods this is not a conscious obedience, and for man it is. To man the Word comes as an address, a confrontation, an impact of person on person. God proclaims and man is called upon to believe; God commands and man is required to obey; God promises and man is invited to trust and depend. The very humanity of man lies in his ability thus to receive and respond to the Word. His fall is simply his refusal to respond.

The peace of Eden rested on a right relation with God. Once that relation is broken we see the break-up of unity on every level. Man, estranged from God, turns out to be estranged also from himself: the flesh no longer serves the spirit but becomes disorderly and a temptation, and man finds himself naked. He is estranged from nature, and the ground brings forth thistles. Man and wife are estranged from one another, and bandy accusations against one another. The alienation is progressive, and as the numbers of mankind increase so does their discord. Before the family has expanded into a village community a murder has been committed, and generations later the invention of metallurgy leads to the production of weapons and the intensification of the blood feud. Thereafter, throughout the biblical history, this same ambivalence clings about all the doings of men. It is not that they are incapable of

16

finding any truth or doing anything righteous, but that every truth breeds fresh error and every just institution is twisted to unjust uses. God has so made the world that, when we try to live without respect to His laws, this is what happens. It is a natural necessity and it is also the judgment of God.

At the same time our relations with God Himself are poisoned and perverted. He who spoke to us invitingly as a Father was also our King. His wisdom should have been our light and His power our protection. Now we have defied Him, but we have not thereby got rid of him. We have only thrown away our trust in His protection and learned instead to fear His power. We might have stood before Him as beloved children, but instead we stand before Him as guilty men before their judge or as captured rebels before their legitimate sovereign. The Word still speaks, but now it speaks in judgment and in condemnation. 'The Word of God is living and active and sharper than any two-edged sword, piercing even to the dividing of soul and spirit, of both joints and marrow, and quick to discern the thoughts and intents of the heart.' It forces us to face the consequences of our wrong choice. Having flouted God's good will, we are banished from His fellowship and left to our quarrels with ourselves and one another.

From the beginning man has laboured to heal this breach. The history of religion is the history of man's attempts to build a bridge back to God. But if we look again at the sacred story we see there that the first recorded sacrifice becomes the occasion of a fratricidal murder. Such is the Bible's verdict on man's religious endeavours. The just man's sacrifice may be accepted for the sake of the just man who offers it; the unjust man's offering cannot cure or cover up his injustice. And this of course is as it must be so long as men, who broke with God in order to follow their own notions, think they can restore communion with Him on their own terms and by their own contrivances.

2. THE CORRUPTION OF MAN'S NATURE

Man cannot obey God's Word if he cannot understand it. A responsible being must be an intelligent being, and to be responsible to God he must be able to understand what God says and wills. Nor can he rule over nature if he cannot understand its laws, and to do this is again in a manner to understand God, since the laws of nature are an expression of the divine wisdom. The Old Testament shows us the wisdom of God present with Him before creation and working with Him in the creation.

> 'Then I was by him, as a master-workman:
> And I was daily his delight,
> Rejoicing always before him;
> Rejoicing in his habitable earth;
> And my delight was with the sons of men.'[1]

The New Testament, in speaking of Christ as the 'Word' of God, uses a term which also means 'reason'; it thus allows us to think of Him as the Light of Reason eternally present with God, active in the creation and lightening every man by its coming into the world. It was no mere private whim that made Justinian dedicate his great cathedral in the name of the Holy Wisdom, and set himself up as a rival to the Israelite king who was both a temple-builder and a model of wisdom. And as all the creation of God manifests His wisdom, so among the gifts of His Spirit a high place is given to wisdom and understanding.

We see therefore why there is a Christian tradition which finds the divine image in man in man's intelligence. Man is capable of knowing God and incapable of true happiness without knowing Him. Man is made for the contemplation of Him in whose image he is made; all his thoughts, all his perceptions and all his actions should work together to feed that contemplation or should flow from it as acts of love and

[1] Proverbs 8.30.

worship. So living in the vision and love of God, man will become conformed to what he knows and loves, and his whole being will become a 'reasonable, holy and lively sacrifice' to God.

This state is not to be reached without effort and discipline. It involves a continual battle against the distractions of daily life and a progressive focussing of the mind upon God, who alone is the truth, who alone can truly say I AM. Christian tradition again has marked out the steps of the ladder by which we rise to the contemplation of God. We begin with the things around us, the material things and processes of Nature. We begin by seeing these as they should be seen, not as brute facts or random happenings, but as acts of God, as manifestations of His nature. From material things we rise to an understanding of the immaterial, of the powers of the human soul and of the angelic intelligences which see God so much more nearly than we do. From the knowledge of created spirits again we rise to trace the work of God in their lives, His judgments, His providences, His manifold gifts of grace. From these again we pass to Christ, who is the source and centre of all creation, and in Himself a complete and perfect manifestation of the Father. All creation flows from Him and points back to Him. All grace is given through Him and unites us with Him. No one can see the Father except in the Son, nor approach the Father except by the way which the Son has opened. On the other hand, to see the Son Himself aright we must know that He is the Word of the Father, made flesh by the operation of the Spirit. So from His flesh we pass to the eternal Word who wears that flesh, and so to the Blessed Trinity, before whom the intellect falls blinded, but in whom the will finds its perfect rest. Such is the Christian discipline of the intellect; such is the *itinerarium mentis ad Deum*.

If man was created to know the truth and to enjoy the real, his falling away must consist in believing a lie and embracing fantasies. Such is indeed the nature of the fall. It began not with us but with one of the angelic princes, who, although in possession of the clear vision of God, shut his eyes to the light and committed himself to that lie which is the source of all other lies: 'I am (or I can be) independent like God.' The acceptance of this lie brings immediate ruin over the whole field of thought. That field loses its true centre and is refocussed upon a false centre, upon the liar himself. Everything is thereby twisted out of due proportion and perspective. The intellect loses the good for which it was made, and wearies itself in vain attempts to find a satisfaction which always eludes it, and when the intellect has lost its proper good, so also has the will. Refusing to love God, we are compelled to fix our love upon something other than God, but since our capacity for love is infinite, nothing other than God can satisfy it. Therefore the fallen will, like the fallen intellect, is afflicted with perpetual hunger and restlessness. Pursuing, as it must, wrong ends instead of the right one, it suffers as much by what it achieves as by what it fails to achieve, since even its achievements confirm it in the false belief that there is satisfaction along that road. Self-frustration is the law of all action that is divorced from the love of God.

The deterioration is progressive. False beliefs and systems of belief become established as an inseparable part of our cultural inheritance, false aims and perverted institutions propagate themselves through history. Within the individual soul the intellect is darkened, the imagination inflamed, the will perverted and subdued to the passions. Man lives as the ruin of what he should have been.

Some consciousness of his unhappy state man has always had, but he buoys himself up with the hope of a cure from every source but the right one. He seeks it from wealth, power and knowledge, he seeks it from moral progress, he seeks it from philosophical wisdom and from religion. All of these promise peace but give none; they shed a troubled and a darkened light. St. Anselm in the opening section of his *Proslogion* states the position clearly. God, he says, invites me to seek His face. I ask nothing better, for to this end I was created; but how can I seek when I do not know how or where to seek? My mind is darkened, and I cannot do the thing for which I was made, and without which I can know no real joy. From lamentation over his fallen state Anselm passes gradually into a prayer for light and for the power to apprehend this light. He was made in God's image in order that he might know and love God; and God's image must be renewed in him if he is to know and love God as he desires to do. But this renewal only God Himself can bring about.

3. FRUSTRATION OF FUNCTION

From our first and second points taken together follows the third. If man is created capable of knowing and loving God, capable of hearing the Word and living in fellowship with Him who speaks, we can learn from this what function man is meant to perform in the economy of creation. He is in the world that he may glorify God and that the world may glorify God through him. He was placed in the garden to be the gardener, i.e. not to be its master, but to tend it for another. He is given power and authority over all the works of God's hands, but he has this authority in order that through him the works of God may do that for which they were made.

> 'The heavens declare the glory of God,
> And the firmament showeth his handiwork.'

How can they declare it when

> 'There is neither speech nor language,
> Nor any voice that is heard among them'?[1]

They glorify God through man, who sees God's glory in them.

> 'In reason's ear they all rejoice,
> And utter forth a glorious voice.'

[1] Psalm 19.1, 3.

Not what things are in their physical selves, but what they are in the eyes of God's intelligent creatures, is their true meaning, as it is written, 'Whatsoever the man called any living creature, that was the name thereof.'

This means, in a word, that man is nature's priest. Nature is offered up to God on the altar of man's worship. But how can man do this with darkened mind and twisted will, and alienated from God? He not only cannot do it, but he offers false worship instead, false sacrifices to false gods, a misunderstood world misapplied to the fulfilment of misguided purposes. If nature is to glorify God as it was meant to do, if it is to be what it should be and mean what it should mean, its priest must be restored to it. But he cannot restore himself.

4. CAPTIVITY TO SATAN

False gods are no mere fantasy. They are real and dangerous powers. The hosts of evil, who are our leaders and teachers in sin, are also our tyrants in the sinful world which we inhabit. It is for this that they live. Deprived by their own choice of the vision and enjoyment of God, they have no choice left but to seek to satisfy an insatiable hunger by means of power and conquest. Of this conquest we are the chosen victims, and, like many another victim, we lay ourselves open to the aggressor. Every human fantasy which has become fixed in a formula and focussed in an image and is capable of obsessing the mind, every false purpose dwelt upon as a longing, crystallised as a habit and so ruling the will, provides a dwelling-place into which powers more deeply sunk in falsehood and sin than we can enter and dwell. It is thus that a man's unbridled fancies and unchastened desires can lay him open to victorious temptation and sometimes to worse – and what is true of individual men is true also of societies and civilisations.

It is thus that we must analyse all pagan gods. Such gods are a compound of two factors. On the one hand there is a human fantasy, a name, a tradition of addressability, a more or less personal figure with a character and a myth, typifying some characteristic of man or some power of nature, and symbolising some human hope or fear. This is the natural element, the human element in the false gods. This is the *eidolon*. Of this, St. Paul and the Psalmist truly say that it is nothing at all. But on the other hand the fantasy, false and empty in itself, is an open door through which the hostile powers enter in and govern the mind and soul of men and of peoples. And this is the sense in which the Fathers truly say that the gods of the heathen are evil spirits.

Nor is this the only way in which the lords of hell display their power over humanity. Where paganism is dead and the very names of the old gods are forgotten, intellectual, social and political movements serve their purpose no less well, and today the demonic power in these things is clearly manifest.

This is the captivity of man and whether he willingly accepts it and becomes a subject of the evil kingdom, or whether he struggles vainly against it as he feels its degrading pressure, in neither case can he set himself free.

5. PSYCHOLOGICAL RESISTANCES

Sin is a disease, and we have seen how the Bible parallels it with various kinds of physical illness. But our present-day knowledge of mental sickness throws fresh light upon it. Sin has much in common with neurosis. Like neurotic patients, we are fond of our symptoms because they make us interesting and because they make us genuinely unable to do what we profoundly fear to do, i.e. to take the road of health. It is not merely that we will not turn to God. So long as our symptoms remain we can honestly say that we cannot do it; we may even delude ourselves into thinking that this excuses us. The neurotic patient at first resists diagnosis, at least he will welcome and even offer of his own accord false diagnoses, but he resists the true one when it comes over the horizon. And he cannot be treated until this resistance is broken down and he is prepared to face the truth about himself. All this is equally true of the sinner. He too is full of false theories about the cause of his disabilities and unhappinesses; he too offers strong resistance to the true account of his condition. The resistance may take various forms. It may appear as anger or resentment at what he considers an insult to himself. It may take the form of ridicule. It may take the form of the mind going blank, an iron curtain of incomprehension coming down if one probes too near the point.

Behind all these resistances is fear, the fear of self-knowledge; because true self-knowledge involves knowledge of God, and we cannot face the knowledge of God unless we are prepared to renounce everything in us which stands against Him, and that may be almost the whole of our existing selves. In this sense it is true that no man can see God and live; that is, in the light of God's presence that compound of sins and follies which he thinks of and prizes as 'himself' must wither and die. In another sense, of course, the knowledge of God is our only true life and the vision of Him is our eternal joy. But to the sinner *as* sinner eternal life appears not as life at all, but as death, and he defends himself by every means against the threat of it.

It is obvious that these defences cannot be torn down by the very person who is obstinately or desperately erecting them. Reconciliation must come from without. Some other person must inject into us thoughts and motives by which the resistance may be undermined. The process may be long and difficult, and there is no logical certainty in any given case that conciliation will succeed. But without it the man is lost, for the healer cannot begin to do His work.

II

The Five-Fold Solution

THE POSITION is desperate. Man no longer occupies his proper place or performs his proper function. He is no longer truly himself. It is a comprehensive calamity in which we are all involved and from which we cannot escape. For the root of the evil lies in the perversion of the will, and the will which is perverse cannot whole-heartedly will to be sound. We see to some extent the nature of the evil, we struggle feebly against it, but the struggle is always vain, and each attempt at the recovery of virtue breeds new sins. It is a self-perpetuating evil, a world system of evil persisting from generation to generation. It is the 'world' (*kosmos*) in St. John's sense of the word, that world which 'has both seen and hated' the Son and the Father, which hates us who belong to the Son, and which the Son has overcome. It is 'the iron furnace, the house of bondage' in which we are held at once by the power of Satan and by our own fears and ignorances. Our deliverance, therefore, must mean deliverance from the world, an escape from captivity and death, a return to life and freedom. It is thus in fact that the New Testament presents it to us; as a return from far places, as a deliverance from Egypt, or again as a healing of sickness, a new birth, a resurrection from the dead. But these are works which only God can perform. The destruction of satanic power is a work for one who is stronger than men or angels. The restoration of life is a work for Him who gave it.

So much we could learn from the Old Testament alone. The prophets and psalmists knew well enough that Israel's salvation could only come from God. What they did not know

25

is that it was to come through God as man. This, which is the first point of stumbling both for Jew and for Greek, is the first distinctive point of the Christian gospel. God has not saved us by an act of power from a distance. He dwelt among us, became our brother and we therefore His, and what was then done can never be undone. Human nature is seated on the throne of heaven.

What was His purpose in thus coming among us? Partly, no doubt, to be understood. We understand no language but human language. If God is to speak to us, He must speak in this language; and if He is to make known to us His whole counsel, He must not send us messages through a prophet, but come and show Himself and speak to us in person. And again He comes among us to conciliate, to win us by being seen among us in His beauty, by speaking words and doing things to draw the world to Himself. But more than all this, He comes among us to do the work of man as man for man, to restore human nature in His own person and give us back that nature at once restored and glorified.

We have known a kind of Catholicism which has talked as if this were the heart of the gospel; we have been told that Christianity and in particular Catholicism is the religion of the Incarnation. By the mere fact of living among us, God has sanctified our race. By wearing a human body He has declared once and for all the sanctity of matter and put an end to the dreams of the Platonist and the Manichee. He sanctified human labour by participation in it, and on the fact of Christ the carpenter a Christian sociology has been built. All this is true, but this is not yet the full gospel. These are the beginnings of His ways. The Catholic faith is more than this.

The Apostles did not preach a religion of the Incarnation. They preached the Resurrection. Not human life as we know it, not even human life sanctified by His participation in it, but a new life, a risen life was what they preached. We are baptised into Christ not as incarnate, but as dead and risen. Again we commemorate Him, offer Him and receive Him in the Eucharist, not merely as incarnate, but as dead and risen. The Eastern Church delights to see the Resurrection foreshadowed even in the days of His flesh at the moment of transfiguration, where the spokesmen of the Law and the Prophets appear speaking with Him of His coming death which is also His 'Exodus', surrounded by a foretaste of the glory which is to be. And in all parts of Christendom the crown of the year is Easter:

Lady and Queen and Day of days.

We see Him then as Life victorious over death.

Death and life have contended
In the combat stupendous:
The Prince of Life, who died, reigns immortal.

The Apostles preached the Resurrection; but there can be no resurrection unless there has been a death. The Transfiguration, foretelling the glory, declares also that the death comes first; and the body of the risen Lord bears visibly the marks of what He first endured. Without the Resurrection Christ's death would be fruitless, but without the death His exaltation would lose its meaning. In the death, therefore, the Christian mind has come more and more to see the heart of the mystery. The Cross after all has become the symbol of the faith. It is a striking paradox, a conception worthy of a God, that God should not merely live as man but die, and not merely die but be executed, and this by the wisest and noblest religious authority then existing in the world, which yet was not wise enough to know the time of its visitation. This is the decisive judgment, not merely on mankind, but on the Church. And here is another element of the Christian paradox – that the same act by which judgment is brought to a point should also have been the act which brought salvation. Yet the unswerving testimony of the Church has been that this is so, and that the Christ who is the Saviour is Christ crucified.

27

Here is the decisive and truly crucial act on which the Atonement hangs. But then we ask: *how* is it decisive? Why was the Cross necessary, and what did it achieve? The long history of theories of the Atonement springs from these questions. From what evil could He think to deliver us by being crucified? Or (to put the question differently) our situation being what it is, how can He relieve it by being crucified? By being incarnate, yes. By being exalted and glorified, yes. He who is Life itself thus brings new life to those who are dead. But how does His own death contribute to our life? These are not merely questions agitated among scholars. In every generation there are those among the faithful who press these questions upon us anew. The problem of the Atonement is a real and recurring problem, and at its heart is the question: why a cross?

Death is an unpleasant thing, violent death more so, death by unjust violence more so still. The physical sufferings inflicted by crucifixion are known to be very great; while of the spiritual suffering of the crucified God the New Testament gives us a distant hint. The whole episode from His arrest to His death is commonly known as the 'Passion', i.e. the suffering. Hence it is not surprising that the opinion should have become widespread that the virtue of His crucifixion lay precisely in the pain of it. Phrases occur in the Bible and in well-known hymns which appear on the surface to mean just this.

> *But the pains which He endured*
> *Our salvation have procured.*

The problem of the Atonement then takes on a peculiar form. Christ has delivered us from death and suffering and He has done this by His own death and suffering; but in what way, by what kind of legal or moral or spiritual exchange, can His endurance of what He never deserved save me from having to endure what I have deserved? The sufferings of Christ on the

Cross come to be thought of as in some way an equivalent for or counterpoise to the pains of hell, which all humanity has deserved to suffer.

It is recorded that Schleiermacher, as a schoolboy, spent much time trying to puzzle out by what scale of measurement the sufferings of Christ could equal the sufferings from which He releases us, or contain a virtue sufficient to purchase our release. Schleiermacher is not alone in having asked this question. Too many theories of the Atonement have been constructed as answers to it. There is no satisfactory answer, and there need not be, because the question itself is the wrong one. The assumption on which it rests, *viz.* that the saving factor in the death of Christ is what He suffered, considered precisely as suffering, as pain, is unproven and untrue. There is no ground for it in Scripture and there is no ground for it in reason. The merit of His death, as we shall see, lies not in the pain, but in the unswerving obedience, of which the willing acceptance of that pain was merely the crowning proof. The obedience of the second Adam cancels the disobedience of the first, and is the beginning of our salvation as that was the beginning of our loss.

The Incarnation itself was His first great act of obedience. That obedience was then carried on into everything said, done or undergone in the whole course of His earthly life. The Cross itself was obedience carried to the point beyond which it could not be carried any further, obedience to the point of self-annihilation. And thus we return in a new fashion to the doctrine which we seemed but now to reject. It is after all by His life among us that we are saved, but not by that life merely as present and moving in our midst. It is by that life as obedience, from which the death is inseparable; since if one really sets out in this world, nay even in Israel, to obey God without reservation, one cannot but end in some such way. So the life and the death are all of a piece together, and the Resurrection is the crown of both.

Even this is not enough. For if these things happened once upon a time and are now over and done with, what is that to us? In the words of James Nayler, the seventeenth-century enthusiast, 'He that expecteth to be saved by Jesus Christ that died at Jerusalem shall be deceived.' Certainly, if all He did was to die at Jerusalem, if the Jesus of history is not also the indwelling Christ of every day. Christian devotion dwells continually on the mystical union between Christ and the believing soul. All that is His is ours. The Christian life is described now as His life in us and now as our life in Him. He is born in us, lives, works, suffers and dies in us and rises in us to the glorified life; or alternatively we are reborn in Him, live, work, suffer, die and rise again in Him. Both images are Pauline, both are Johannine. The believer is in Christ and Christ in him: the two together are, in Luther's words, 'one cake, one bread, one body'.

Only so can the alienation of man from God be overcome and man return to the divine unity. In Christ's obedience, in His sonship, in His life and virtue and power, man becomes again what he should be and takes again the place which should be his. We must now trace this out in detail under our five headings.

I. RENEWAL OF FELLOWSHIP

We have broken fellowship with God and are in a state of alienation from Him. Here there are two things to be distinguished, a cause and an effect. We have offended against God and continually do offend and in consequence of this we are excluded from His fellowship. Our deliverance from this state must therefore itself include two elements: a negative one, the cancelling of the offence, and a positive one, the restoration of fellowship.

The Bible has a wealth of terms to describe both of these processes. To begin with the negative aspect, we read of sins being 'covered up', or 'blotted out', or 'taken away', or 'purged'; or again God is said to 'pass over' the sins of His people and to remember them no more. All these are simply synonyms for cancellation; they signify that the offence is abolished and they tell us no more than that.

Richer in meaning is the Greek word *aphesis*, whose equivalent in Latin is *remissio* and in English 'forgiveness'. *Aphienai* is to let go; the judge 'lets go' the lawful penalty or the creditor 'lets go' the debt, i.e. he refrains from exacting it, or the offended person 'dismisses' the offensive act, i.e. he puts it out of mind. To forgive is to give up, to give away, to concede, i.e. to abandon a lawful claim in favour of someone else, and to remit is much the same. St. Paul also uses a more colourful word than these, *viz. charizesthai*, to give a present or to grant a favour. God, he says, 'makes us a present' of our sins, i.e. He 'lets us get away with' them. All these terms belong together in one family. Their basic meaning is still negative, the cancellation of our offence; but they also indicate that this cancellation is an act of free grace on the part of God.

The Bible does not often connect remission or forgiveness of sins with the person of Christ or with His death. The passage in Matthew 26.28, which is so familiar to us through its use in the liturgies, is really something of an exception. The conditions usually laid down for the forgiveness of sins are repentance (with its co-implicates, confession and restoration) and readiness to forgive. Christ Himself bids us pray to be forgiven 'as we forgive'. But then He also tells us that unless we forgive 'from our hearts' we shall not receive forgiveness, and to those who begin to know their own hearts this is one of the most frightening texts in Scripture. We cannot fulfil the condition so long as we remain what we are. We can do it only as we are transformed into the likeness of Christ, we living in Him and He in us; and so it is that in the end there is no remission of sins except through Him.

But the remission of sins is only the beginning of the gospel.

31

It is the negative side of it, the cancellation of the offence; but what of the positive side, the restoration of unity between God and man? Here too the Bible is rich in words and images to describe it. The most famous of them is of course that of the prodigal's return: he is not merely allowed to slip back home and no questions asked, he is welcomed with open arms and made the centre of festivity. Or we may think of the return of the erring wife to her husband, who has not only redeemed her from slavery and disgrace, but gives her back her youth and greets her as a bride. Or, to pass from imagery to sober historical fact, it is the transformation of enemies into friends, of sinners into saints, of persecutors into apostles and martyrs.

These are striking and memorable conceptions, full of meaning, but can we not analyse their meaning and see more in detail what is involved? St. Paul is our principal analyst, with St. John operating effectively in support. To St. Paul we owe the doctrine of justification, of which I shall speak at length in my fourth lecture. Here I will only say that this word, justification, has a far richer meaning than the mere remission of sins. On the one hand it means reinstatement, the restoration of the sinner to that status in God's family which he has forfeited by his sin and which, although forgiven, he still does not deserve. On the other hand it also means the gradual transformation of his character into something which fits his status as a child of God. Another Pauline word is 'reconciliation', which means the restoration of friendly relations and intercourse between those who have been estranged. With these must be connected the freedom of speech (*parrhesia*) of which St. Paul speaks once and St. John more often: the confidence with which in Christ we can approach the Father, not merely as subjects or servants but as beloved children. The conception of Christ as the peace-maker also belongs to this group; for His peace is not merely the cessation of strife and the removal of hostilities, but the breaking down of all barriers, even those of mere distance or difference, and the bringing together of all mankind in one family.

Here as before it must be acknowledged that we owe these benefits to Christ alone, and this time the Bible is quite explicit about it. If we appear in God's household not as slaves but as sons, it is because the Son has set us free. If we confidingly address our Lord and King as our Father, it is because the Spirit of the Son so speaks in us. If we receive from the Father's hands so much more than we deserve, it is because He is pleased to see in us not the sinful creatures that we are in ourselves, but members of the mystical body of His Son. For he who is in Christ, so far as he is in Christ, cannot be a sinner. Made one with the Son, he is made one with the obedience of the Son, even to the cross which is the crown of that obedience. The disastrous legacy of the Tree of Knowledge is cancelled in him by the virtue of the Tree of Victory, and in union with the second Adam he re-enters that Eden from which, with the first Adam, he had been expelled.

2. RESTORATION OF HUMAN NATURE

St. Athanasius remarks (*De Incarnatione*, 7) that, if there were nothing between us and God except an occasional act of sin, we might reasonably be forgiven and restored to favour simply on repentance for that sin. But, he goes on, our situation is far worse than that. We have not merely acted wrongly; we have undergone a corruption of our very nature. We have lost the image of God and the grace which should go with it. To be restored, we must be given back what we have lost, and that means nothing less than that He who first created us must now 'recreate' us and bring us back from corruption to incorruption. This is not a simple process, it has a variety of aspects, and to each of them in its due place the Bible and Christian tradition do justice.

First of all, the corruption of our nature can be regarded as a sickness or even as a death. Its restoration therefore is healing, or it is a gift of new life. The latter in turn can be thought of in two alternative ways: it is a new birth, or it is a resurrection from the death of sin. With these biblical images we may couple the phrase of St. Ignatius when he describes the Holy Communion as the 'medicine which makes immortal'. The idea and equivalent phrases can be traced through the whole history of eucharistic devotion. The remembrance that every Sunday is a little Easter should keep this view of the matter constantly before us.

But secondly, the core of man's nature lies in his will. From the corruption of the will destruction spreads over the rest of man's life. Sin is this corruption, it is not error or ignorance but sheer ill will. Therefore in the restoration of human nature a special place must be given to the restoration of the will. And this in turn has three aspects. It has a negative aspect, the purging of the will, the stripping away of sinful impulses and habits. It has a positive aspect, the gift of righteousness, the imparting to the soul of the different virtues one by one, and at last the union of them all in the perfect virtue of love. And thirdly, beyond even this, there is that steadfast adherence and dedication of the will to God which constitutes holiness. What are the biblical terms for these things? The gift of righteousness is part of what is meant by St. Paul's word 'justification'; but towering above it stands the gift of holiness, or 'sanctification', without which our hold upon righteousness itself is insecure. This distinction between the two terms is not always clearly drawn, but I believe that something is lost where it is neglected. We may find an allusion to it in that beautiful post-communion hymn of the Slavonic liturgies: 'Preserve us in Thy holiness, that so we may learn of Thy righteousness.'

Thirdly, side by side with the restoration of the will goes that of the intellect. The Old Testament has much to say about our coming to 'know' God, and St. John is never tired of speaking of the divine gifts of light and truth. All these are

terms whose meaning goes beyond mere intellectual appre-
hension, but at the same time quite certainly includes it. In the
list of the seven gifts of the Spirit, which Western Christendom
has associated with Confirmation, it is noteworthy that four
out of the seven are intellectual gifts, and in St. Paul's great list
in 1 Corinthians 12, wisdom and knowledge stand at the head
of them all. Similarly the neophyte in his baptism is said to be
'enlightened', and baptism itself in some passages of the Fathers
appears to be referred to as the 'illumination' (*photismos*). In
my previous lecture I referred to St. Anselm's *Proslogion* to
show how he felt the darkening of the intellect and the frustration springing from that. The *Proslogion* continues with a
prayer to God to grant him light, to 'renew' and 'restore' his
fallen nature, in order that he may understand what he already,
by God's grace, knows and believes.

Fourthly, human nature thus restored is not merely made
sound, it is made incorruptible. Immortality and incorrupti-
bility are constant themes of Greek theology, and so is the
deification (*theosis, theopoiesis*) which is the end of the spiritual
road. There is scriptural warrant for this in II Peter 1.4, which
speaks of our 'becoming partakers in a (or the) divine nature';
and if in recent centuries the Western Church, for intelligible
reasons, has often fought shy of the use of these words, we can
still read in St. John of the Cross that the contemplative soul
'becomes God by participation'.

Nothing of all this can take place otherwise than through the
work of Christ in us. In His Person the image of God is
restored to humanity, and that in a fuller sense than it was first
given to Adam. From His human nature, imparted to us in
baptism and nourished in us by holy communion, we derive
our power to think and will aright, our wisdom, our righteousness, our holiness. Our triumph over corruption and death
and our participation in the divine nature are ours through Him.
There is no need to dwell further upon this, for of course we
all know it. However one may analyse in detail the work of

Christ for us and in us, one must always at last sum it up and draw it together in the simple formula: 'He in us and we in Him.'

3. RESTORATION OF FUNCTION

Christ in His earthly obedience offered Himself to the Father; and His death on the Cross, which is the crown of that obedience, is also the moment at which His offering is consummated and becomes the perfected sacrifice. All humanity and all creation, summed up in Him, is in a manner offered there, and in His continuing High-priestly work in heaven He, perfect man, does perfetlcy what man was created to do as the priest of all creation. But we, His members, who share His nature, share also His sacrificial function, and are one with Him both in offering and in being offered.

The New Testament in several places speaks of the Christian people as an offering made to God. We, or our worship and service, are described as a sacrifice (*thysia, prosphora*). We are a 'sweet savour' in God's nostrils – an Old Testament term for sacrifice. More interesting is the fact that St. Paul, in speaking of his ministry in bringing the nations to God, describes it as a liturgy (*leitourgia*). He speaks of 'the grace which was given to me by God, that I might be a *leitourgos* of Christ Jesus towards the Gentiles, ministering (*hierourgounta*) the Gospel of God, in order that the offering (*prosphora*) of the Gentiles may be acceptable, being sanctified by the Holy Ghost'.

In these passages we, the Christian people, are spoken of as that which is offered. But we are also those who offer. Even in the Old Testament it was clear that God's people, whom He had chosen and redeemed, were a priestly people. In a similar spirit St. John declares that God 'has made us a kingdom and priests'. Indeed the word *hiereus* is never applied in the New Testament to the ministers of the Church as a distinct order within it, but only to the whole body of the faithful.

Although in subsequent centuries the conception of priesthood has come to be connected much more closely with those who celebrate the liturgy, dispense the sacraments, and exercise spiritual oversight in the Church, the liturgies themselves have not ceased to contain the affirmation that the eucharistic sacrifice is offered by the whole body of the faithful who are present at it. And as all the prayers of the Church cluster around that supreme prayer, it follows that all the faithful, whenever they pray as Christians, in Christ and therefore in the Church, are in their degree performing a priestly act.

As we are the offering and the offerant, so also we are the temple. Christ is the true Temple, the Bethel, over which the heavens stand open and the angels of God ascend and descend; and we who are His members are also the living stones of the Temple which is His Body. It is a Temple not made with hands, erected and consecrated by the Holy Ghost for the offering of spiritual sacrifices, for the worshipping of the Father in spirit and in truth; and they bring the glory of all the nations into it.

4. OUR DELIVERANCE FROM SATAN

We fell under Satan's power by yielding to his suggestions. Suggestion is his only weapon against us, but it suffices to hold us in slavery, since there is always something in us which welcomes and yields to it. Our freedom therefore can only be won by successful resistance to his suggestions; and the problem is, how this resistance can be set up. Of ourselves we cannot do it, for though we often wish to resist, we do not wish it wholeheartedly. Successful resistance could be offered only by someone free from the internal weakness which is original sin, someone who can say as Christ did say, 'the Prince of this world is coming but he has no foothold in me', and who can therefore meet the full force of temptation without yielding. The battle with the enemy runs right through Our Lord's life, reaching its climax in the willing acceptance of the Cross, and thereafter the tempter has nothing more that he can do. He has shot his last bolt, unavailingly. In Christ therefore there now exists what never existed before, a human nature fully tested and yet virtuous and intact. Into this human nature we are incorporated, and our incorporation into the victor is our liberation from the vanquished.

It should go without saying that liberation in this context does not mean independence. For created spirits there is no real independence. The false promise of it is the lure by which we are brought under Satan's tyranny. But the only alternative to this false freedom which is in fact slavery is the willing service of God. The life which Christ victoriously lived was a life of unswerving obedience to the Father. It is in this service that we find our freedom, and the Apostle who tells us to 'stand fast in the freedom wherewith Christ has set us free' is the same who describes himself in the headings of his letters as the 'slave of Jesus Christ'.

Our deliverance from Satan appears in Scripture under various forms of presentation. It appears as the victory of Christ over the tempter and over that organised mass of evil of which he is the prince. 'Be of good cheer, I have overcome the world'; and because He has overcome the world, it is also said of us that we 'have overcome the evil one'. This victory is also represented as our deliverance from Egypt. All this is quite straightforward. But elsewhere we read of a 'redemption' and the paying of a 'ransom'. Here we have an image which can be and often has been misleadingly interpreted. One pays a ransom to deliver a prisoner of war, or someone kidnapped by brigands. In the case of the prisoner of war, the captor has a recognised right to claim ransom. It is his by the law of nations. But Satan has no right to claim ransom for us. We were not captured in legitimate warfare, and there is no *jus gentium* between the City of God and the City of the Devil. In the case of the brigands, they extort the ransom from someone unwilling, while themselves incurring no loss. But Satan extorts nothing from God and himself undergoes defeat. Our salvation has nothing in common with the paying of a ransom except this, that we are delivered from slavery at a great personal cost to the deliverer. It would have been well if the analogy had never been pressed beyond this point.

5. THE BREAKING DOWN OF RESISTANCES

The fifth aspect of the Saviour's work is the breaking down of our resistances, the barriers which we ourselves raise against the would-be healer and reconciler. In this part of His work Christ appears as an ambassador from the Father, bringing a message of conciliation. He invites us, He draws us, He charms us, as Clement of Alexandria says, like a better and nobler Orpheus. And here His relation to us is in a manner more external than we have hitherto found it, for His appeal is made in the first instance to our eyes and ears and minds, through what He says and does and undergoes. No doubt it is true that we could not properly understand His appeal or respond to it but for the secret work of grace within; but still it is to the conscious mind that the appeal is made, and only through it to the will. We are moving more on the psychological than on the mystical level here.

The conception of God 'drawing' us is found in both the Old and the New Testament. 'I have drawn them with bands of love' says God through Hosea (11.4). 'Draw me after thee, let us run' says the Bride to the Bridegroom in the Canticle. 'I, if I be lifted up, will draw all men unto Me' says the incarnate Lord. By what does He draw? By His beauty. And wherein lies His beauty? Not in physical form or feature, not in the words which He speaks, taken simply as words, but in the mighty acts of His birth, life, passion and resurrection. To some, it is the child in the manger who exercises the strongest appeal; to some it is the young man crucified, or the king who reigns from the tree. Upon the contemplation of these two things, the manger and the cross, Bethlehem and Calvary, Christian devotion feeds and Christian evangelism is based. It is the immense condescension of God who becomes man, and who even as man lives in obscurity, slandered, persecuted, put to death on a false charge with every circumstance of pain and disgrace. But it is also the unconquerable patience of Him who endures all this, and after it all is with us more powerfully and more intimately even than before. He sent His messengers and we killed them. He came Himself and we killed him. There is nothing more that we can do. But He returns from the dead, glorious and strong and wholly undiscouraged, and the voice which we thought we had silenced fills the world and pierces the soul. This immeasurable humility and patience, this ability to receive the full impact of hatred and indifference and go on undeterred, is the strongest of the cords by which He draws us.

It is here that we see the foundation and the force of the Abelardian theory of the Atonement. The winning power of Christ, His power to break down indifference and ill will and bring us to the point where we are willing to let Him have His way with us: this is what impressed Abelard. In an age when all France was busy discussing the different forms of love, here Abelard saw divine love. It is an indispensable part of the economy of our salvation, it is something to which the evangelist in particular must constantly recur, and upon which meditative devotion may profitably dwell. But of course it is only the beginning of the story. It is not the healing, it is only the winning of the patient's consent to be healed. If it is presented as the whole story of the Atonement, of course it is a false story. And Abelard has in fact the appearance of so presenting it. There can be no doubt that in his own mind he took a disproportionate interest in this side of the matter – foreshadowing the less helpful forms of modern pietism – and in his utterances he gave it an almost exclusive prominence.

St. Bernard, whose appreciation of the winning power of Christ far outstrips Abelard on his own ground, also understood the deeper things which Abelard slurs over; and whatever may be said of his methods as a controversialist or a heresy-hunter, in substance his judgment on Abelard in this matter was the right one.

III

Expiation, Satisfaction, Substitution

THE ACCOUNT of our salvation given in the two previous
lectures was documented from Scripture, and could be as well
documented from the Fathers, the liturgies and the devotional
literature of Christendom. I do not think it can be seriously
questioned that it was a true account of the salvation of man
as the Church has conceived it, preached it and celebrated it.
And yet it did not include some of the words and phrases
which have appeared most frequently in formal theories of the
Atonement, especially in the last eight hundred years. The
'plan of salvation', which was the substance of so many ser-
mons and passionate appeals made by and to our Protestant
forefathers, was conceived in other terms than these. In Roman
Catholic literature too, at least since the Council of Trent,
statements and expositions can be found which have more in
common with classical Protestantism than with the biblical
and patristic doctrine which I have so far expounded. The
ruling conceptions here are those of guilt, anger, punishment
or penalty, expiation, propitiation and satisfaction. The ideas
of law and justice, and also of sacrifice, are brought into connection with these. Taken singly, all these ideas can be found
in the Bible. God's law, God's righteousness, God's wrath are
fundamental biblical themes. In the Mosaic legislation, in the
sacred history and in our Lord's parables we see the punishment
of the guilty. The New Testament speaks of Christ as a propitiation (*hilasmos*) and a sin-offering (*peri hamartias*). All this
is clear. What is not so clear is the merit of a theory which
singles out these things from the rest of the biblical material,

42

interprets and combines them in a certain way, and treats the result as a true and full account of the Atonement. I shall try to show that the theory in question is not a legitimate child of the biblical revelation, but arises from the imputation to God of attitudes and modes of behaviour on which the Bible stands in judgment.

This whole cycle of ideas relates to the first of our original five points – the estrangement between man and God. It is an attempt to show how that estrangement arose and how it can be overcome. Let us therefore begin by considering in general how estrangements arise, according to this view.

It is presupposed that there is someone (the offender) who is under obligation to someone else (the offended person). The obligation includes the duty to obey a law or a legitimate command, and also the duty to show respect or reverence. Estrangement occurs because the offender does not do these things. The situation which so arises may be said to contain four elements.

1. A law has been broken or a legitimate command has been disobeyed.

2. Guilt has been incurred. Note that by 'guilt' in this connection is not meant what psychologists nowadays call guilt, i.e. the feeling of guilt or self-condemnation, nor on the other hand what is meant by the word 'guilty' in a jury's verdict, i.e. 'he committed the offence'. By 'guilt' in the present connection is meant a condition of ill will, of which the offence is merely the outward manifestation.

3. An affront has been administered to the offended person, whose honour has suffered in his own esteem, or in the eyes of others, or both.

4. In consequence of this the offended person becomes estranged from the offender. This estrangement need not mean that he conceives real ill will towards the offender, but it is likely to imply anger or resentment, and it certainly implies

the refusal of those small friendly offices which are normal between people who are on good terms with one another.

The healing of such an estrangement is a double process; it involves expiation, i.e. the purging of the offence, and propitiation, i.e. the conciliation of the offended person. Let us consider how this double process can be brought about.

1. The broken law or flouted command must be vindicated, i.e. it must somehow be able to get its own back on the offender. The offender must fail, and be seen to fail, to get off scot free. The means by which this is brought about is called a penalty, which is sometimes said to be 'inflicted' on the offender, sometimes 'paid' by him. It is something which he is made to do or to undergo to his own loss.

2. Guilt, i.e. ill will, calls not merely for penalty but for punishment. This is a more serious matter. The purpose of punishment I take to be to destroy or injure or banish the guilty person, or if not the person, then at least the guilt that is in him. In human practice punishments vary widely in character and in severity, but all, I think, have this in common, that they are felt to be demanded not so much by the act which constitutes the offence as by the guilty mind from which it springs, and at their heart is the notion of beating down the evil will, destroying it or rendering it impotent.

3. Reparation must be made. Reparation is not restoration, i.e. the giving back of goods or advantages illegitimately obtained. Reparation is a salve for wounded honour. A common word meaning the same thing is 'satisfaction', and another synonym is 'making amends'.

Penalty, punishment and reparation are three aspects of one and the same process, namely expiation. But 4, there must also be propitiation. The offended person must cease to be estranged and cease to hold the offender at a distance. This does not necessarily require a distinct act over and above those already enumerated; the offended person may be propitiated by the same acts by which the offence is expiated. But he can also sometimes be propitiated by an appeal made directly to his good will.

I have described the situation and its requirements as these appear in relations between man and man. Some elements in this analysis undoubtedly apply as between God and man, and theories of the Atonement have too easily assumed that they all apply. On that assumption our relation to God as sinners is this: we must pay a penalty appropriate and adequate to our wrong-doings, we must undergo punishment adequate to our guilt, we must make satisfaction adequate to the affront which we administer to God's honour, and by these means or by direct appeal to His mercy we must propitiate Him.

If this is the situation in which we find ourselves, it is clearly an impossible one. We cannot do any of the things which are required. Hence arises the problem of salvation as conceived by this type of atonement theory. If we are to be saved, one of two things must happen. Either we must somehow be enabled to do what is needed, or we must be let off, it must be remitted to us. And this in turn may happen in one of two ways: it may be remitted to us unconditionally, or because it is done for us by someone else. This last possibility is the one which atonement theorists embrace. Christ saves us by doing for us what we could never do for ourselves. He pays the penalty for our offences and so vindicates the law of God and His justice in enforcing it; He bears the punishment for our guilt; He makes satisfaction to the offended Father, whom by these means He propitiates.

To a different but closely related thought-world belongs the conception of Christ's death as the payment of a debt. This can be interpreted in two ways. Firstly we may say that all creatures owe a debt of worship and obedience to their creator. Man, now fallen, cannot discharge this debt, but Christ as representative Man, 'federal Head of all mankind' in Charles

Wesley's words, discharges it for him. Secondly sin, or rather the penalty of sin, may be regarded as a debt which the sinner has incurred. This too he cannot pay, and Christ pays it for him. The conception of Christ as our 'surety', which one meets not infrequently in Wesley's hymns, seems to belong to this context. He stands guarantor for the payment of our debt.

These theories have in common the conception of Christ as doing something 'for' us, and by 'for' they mean 'instead' of us. What foundation is there in Scripture for this? To tell the truth, very little. There is quite a lot of *hyper*, on behalf of, but very little of *anti*, instead of. The most striking passage is that in which the Son of Man Himself declares that He has come 'to give His life as a ransom in place of many'. But it is probable that the word *anti* here is merely part of the image of the ransom. He who holds the prisoner accepts the ransom price instead of him. But since, as we have seen, the image of the ransom is not to be pressed very far, the idea of a substitution in this passage need not be taken too seriously either. Thus the chief scriptural support of the substitution theory turns out to be weak. Nevertheless in the history of Christian devotion, and still more in the history of soteriology, the idea of substitution has played an important part, and it has usually been interpreted on the lines of the theories which we are now considering: that Christ's obedience and Christ's sufferings are accepted in place of ours.

> For the sheep the Lamb hath bled,
> Sinless in the sinner's stead.

This is the theory of 'vicarious atonement', which, as we shall shortly see, raises very grave difficulties when we pursue its implications. Yet it is so widespread and so persistent, and (may we add?) it awakens such echoes in the soul that it can hardly be without a core of vital truth, however hard it may be to formulate it satisfactorily. We shall have to see what justice we can do to it later on.

There is yet another conception which has close links with the type of theory now under discussion, the conception of the death of Christ as a sacrifice. Sacrifice we have met before in the third of our five points; but there it meant the offering by man of nature and of man himself as a 'sacrifice of praise and thanksgiving' to God. Here on the other hand it is the offering of Christ by Christ as a sacrifice for the sin of man. Two things should be noticed here. This sacrifice is a propitiatory one, not merely a thankoffering but a 'satisfaction for the sins of the whole world'; and it is the death of the victim which in some way has this atoning power. It does not follow from this, but it has often been believed, that the victim dies as a substitute for us, and if that view is taken the doctrine of the sacrifice of Calvary becomes merely one more variety of the vicarious atonement theory. 'Sacrifice' in fact is then merely a picturesque way of saying what we have already said more precisely in our analysis of expiation and propitiation.

Both in the Bible and in Christian devotion the death of Christ is constantly spoken of as a sacrifice, and as there are many sacrifices and types of sacrifice alluded to in the Old Testament, the death of Christ is presented in a variety of ways. It is the killing of the Paschal Lamb. It is the covenant sacrifice of Exodus 24. It is the great sacrifice of the Day of Atonement. Sometimes elements from different parts of the Jewish sacrificial system are brought together with a light-hearted disregard for historical accuracy, as in the words of a well-known hymn:

> *Paschal Lamb, by God appointed,*
> *All our sins on Thee were laid.*

The effect is impressive, and one does not stop to remember that the sins of Israel were never laid on the Paschal Lamb and that the beast on which they were laid, the scapegoat, was not sacrificed. Despite such inaccuracies this kind of language speaks to the soul, and any adequate account of the Atonement must be able to do justice to it. If the theory we are now dis-

47

cussing is rejected, we must find other means of justifying the sacrificial language.

It is a feature of all these vicarious theories that the relation which they postulate between Christ and those whom He saves is a somewhat external one, quasi-legal or even quasi-commercial in character, and far removed from that mystical union between Christ and the believer on which our previous account of salvation was based. These theories give in fact no explanation of how the second, third, and fourth of our original five points could be dealt with. They concentrate attention wholly on the first point, and we shall shortly see that they give no adequate account even of that. How then did they come to have so strong a hold on the Christian mind? I suspect that one factor contributing to this result may have been the spread of a peculiar form of Christocentric devotion. From early mediaeval times there grew up, at least in Western Christendom, a fashion of imaginative and emotional meditation on the humanity of Christ, with special concentration on the circumstances of His passion. Such a form of meditation can be a powerful stimulus to the imitation of Christ, and can lead through that and beyond it to a desire for a more intimate union with Him. One sees this especially in Catholic devotional writers and practices. But it can equally well develop in a different way. I may concentrate my attention not so much on the beauty and majesty of what Christ has done, as on the fact that He has done it for me. The result of this is likely to be, first of all, a deep sense of security and assurance, then an outburst of gratitude, thanksgiving and praise, and finally a strong desire to preach Christ to other people. This is a characteristically 'evangelical' pattern of response. I do not suggest that these two patterns cannot coexist in the same soul, nor do I say that either is necessarily better or truer than the other. Nevertheless they are different, and in the post-Reformation period, especially in Protestant circles, it is the second which has been the more widely diffused. Nor do I think it can be denied that, as compared with the first pattern, it leaves the relation between Christ and the believer on a more transactional level, and can the more easily go with substitutionary views of the nature of the transaction.[1]

Finally, it is consonant with the substitutionary type of theory that those who hold it should become involved in the question, how the Passion of Christ can be a just equivalent for the penalties from which it saves us. Thus we are told that Christ must contrive somehow to do something beyond His duty; for if He merely did His duty the righteousness so acquired would be needed for His own use, but if He does more than His duty He thus acquires a righteousness to spare which can then, if all the conditions are satisfied, be credited to others who need it. And, since the slightest sin is an offence against infinite righteousness, it may be held to be an infinite offence and to demand an infinite penalty. Christ's spare righteousness must therefore be one of infinite worth if it is to do the work for which it is required. Various theories can then arise as to what it is in the death of Christ which has this infinite worth. Truly, if the phrase 'infinite worth' has any meaning in this connection, we can hardly fail to ascribe infinite worth to the merits of Christ; but the way which we have just travelled to reach this obvious conception seems curiously indirect and artificial.

To turn now to criticism of this theory.

The arrangement which it describes is one which might work as between human beings, whose relationships with one another are so often external and artificial. The penalties, for instance, imposed by human law are not the natural consequences of the acts to which they are attached; they are artificial

---

[1] I have borrowed this word from Philip Doddridge:

> *'Tis done, the great transaction's done;*
> *I am my Lord's, and He is mine;*
> *He drew me, and I followed on,*
> *Charmed to confess the voice divine.*

consequences made by the will of man. But what man has ordained man can rescind, and a court of law can readily allow a fine imposed on one person to be paid by another. Similarly the code of honour as between human beings is concerned at least as much with outward word and gesture as with the heart, and it is not inconceivable that an offended person might be appeased by a sufficiently impressive satisfaction offered on behalf of the offender by someone else. But these things are possible precisely because of those features of human relationships which are absent from our relations with God. There nothing is artificial, nothing is superficial. The issue is intimate and personal. It is the whole of man face to face with the whole of God. In this atmosphere it should be immediately evident that legal devices have no place. But let us consider their inadequacy more in detail.

1. I have already said that the penalties imposed by human law are not the natural consequences of our actions, but artificial consequences imposed for reasons of social policy. But God is not a human legislator, He is the lawgiver of the universe, and the 'penalties' which He annexes to human actions are precisely their natural consequences. If the wages of sin is death, it is not because God by a special judicial act inflicts death on a sinner who would otherwise not die, but because sin is itself a mortal disease. But the natural consequences of our actions cannot be finally averted by anything that anyone else does for us, so long as the will from which those actions sprang remains in us unchanged. The consequences can be averted only if our diseased will returns to health, and this return is nothing if it is not our own act.

2. I have said that the aim of punishment is to destroy, neutralise or in some way get rid of the evil will which calls it forth. A human authority animated by this motive may neutralise an offender by imprisoning or deporting him or in extreme cases by putting him to death. Human justice has often to be content with this, since it has few means of counter-

ing the evil will in a more positive way, by converting it into a good one. Yet even among men it is often recognised that this is the better way which should be striven for wherever possible. As for God, He does not will the destruction or even the eternal banishment of the sinner, but rather that he may turn from his wickedness and live. God's way of 'destroying' His enemies is to convert them into friends, and if He 'punishes' the sinner by way of pain or loss it is always in the hope (so long as there remains a hope) that he may be thus converted. For no one does the punishment settle down into irremediable suffering and eternal loss, unless by his own will he becomes eternally fixed in the rejection of God.

3. Bible and Church declare that the death of Christ is a propitiatory sacrifice and a satisfaction rendered to the Father. It follows from this that there is a sense in which the Father requires to be given satisfaction and so propitiated. In what sense can this proposition be true?

It cannot be, as some have strangely supposed, that the Father is wholly lacking in good will towards us, or would be if it were not that the Son in His kindness contrives to change Him. This view is heretical; it is also silly; for it divides the substance. Father and Son are at one in all things. It is the Father who sends the Son to be the Saviour of the world.

Then it must be that the Father, though fundamentally benevolent towards us, is prevented from fully displaying His good will by some obstacle which the death of Christ removes. To justify the use of the words 'satisfaction' and 'propitiation', this obstacle must lie within the Father Himself. It is customary to say that it lies in His justice and in His wrath. And here trouble arises, since both of these divine attributes are easily misunderstood. His justice is conceived as an inflexible will to exact penalties, to inflict punishments, to require satisfaction or reparation. His anger is conceived as a will to destroy the wicked or at least to banish them from His presence for ever. Closer examination will show that these are misconceptions.

(*a*) Justice in the world of men appears most conspicuously in a negative form, as penalising the wrong-doer rather than as establishing right relations between people. So conceived, and embodied in a police force and the majestic trappings of a court of law, it can easily wear a threatening aspect. God as the just judge can appear in the same light. Thus Luther tells us how he used to be frightened by St. Paul's saying about the Gospel, that 'the justice of God is revealed in it'. To him the justice of God was the severity of God, and so the Gospel was no Gospel. Perhaps this is partly a matter of words. The English word 'justice' and the Latin *justitia* do seem to have a connotation of severity and rigorism which is absent from the Hebrew *çedaqa*, the Greek *dikaiosyne*, and our own word 'righteousness'. When the Bible says that God is righteous it means something positive. It means first and foremost that He is the King who establishes and maintains righteousness among His people. What this means for His attitude to sinners we might learn even from Plato, who tells us that it is not the part of the righteous to do harm to the unrighteous, but to make them righteous if he can. God's righteousness in relation to us is His infinite readiness to restore to us the righteousness which we have lost. That is why, in the old Testament, God's righteousness and our salvation are thought of together. Having said this, we can readily go on to admit that He often finds it necessary to smite us in order to save us. What else but this is the core of the prophetic interpretation of history?

(*b*) Again, anger in man is only too often offended dignity. It is self-regarding, a manifestation of wounded pride. That is why human anger is so often destructive and takes the form of a desire to hurt the offender. For this reason many are uneasy at the very thought of connecting anger with God. They should remember that God is not man. It would be too much to say that God has no sense of dignity. He has, and Moses appeals to it when he entreats God not to let Israel perish lest His own good name should suffer thereby. All through the

Bible it is clear that God works unremittingly to manifest His own glory. But it is also clear that God finds His glory in the beatitude of His creatures, and they cannot offend against Him by any act which is not at the same time a serious offence against themselves. We may perhaps find some analogy to God's anger at this sight if we imagine the wholly altruistic anger of nurse or doctor with the patient who obstinately persists in doing what is worst for himself, and in their open disapproval and remedial severity we may see an analogue of the sense in which, while we persist in the folly of sin, God 'turns His face from' us and 'chastises' us.

We know that love and mercy are attributes of God; we know also that justice and anger belong to Him. If what I have just said is right, there can be no thought of an opposition between these two pairs of attributes. On the contrary, the second turns out to be a particular manifestation of the first. But if God shows His justice and seeks His glory in the beatitude of His creatures, it follows that His chastisements will not achieve their end nor His loving wrath be appeased, that (in short) He will not be propitiated, until the beatitude of His creatures is ensured; and nothing can ensure it, short of their own full repentance and their restoration to the state and status from which they have fallen. The idea of a 'satisfaction' made to God by someone other than the offender is thus seen to be inept. There can be no satisfaction but one, and this the offender alone can offer.

Thus, from whatever point of view we regard the matter, we are led to the same conclusion. There can be no remission of penalties, no avoidance of punishment, no satisfaction either for God's wrath or for His justice, short of the full repentance of the sinner himself. And it should be added that, whatever the uncomprehending onlooker may say, the penitent himself finds no difficulty in understanding this. He acknowledges that in himself, as a sinner, he deserves everything that can befall him; he acknowledges also with ever-growing wonder the unmerited goodness of God who works not indulgently, to let him off his deserts, but transformingly, to make him cease to be a sinner. As his repentance becomes more sincere and thorough-going he more and more welcomes the disciplines which God inflicts upon him, seeing in them the means of his purgation and restoration, and he is drawn to take a hand in the process by inflicting disciplinary rigours upon himself. It is to this class of action that the name of penance belongs. Etymologically, of course, there is no difference between penance and penitence; both come from the same Latin source, *poenitentia*, but the existence of the two words in English makes it possible for us to distinguish between penitence, as an inner state, and penance, as a manifestation of it in action.

A penance is a kind of penalty, if not indeed a kind of punishment, and it is curious that moral theory in dealing with the question of punishment has not paid more attention to the significance of penance. The fact that the performance of penances is a regular institution in some religious systems (not only Christian ones) perhaps conceals from some people the fact that it represents a native tendency in mankind. What distinguishes penance from penalty or punishment as generally understood is, I believe, that it is self-inflicted or at least self-sought. Even in those cases where the making of a confession and the performance of a penance are held to be obligatory, it remains true that the penitent asks for a penance, and that the penance which is awarded to him is based on his own self-accusation. We all have this desire, when sorry for what we have done or what we have been, to express this sorrow in word or deed and in some way to penalise ourselves. The motives for this are no doubt mixed. There is the feeling that the performance of such an action helps to crystallise our repentance and to fix our resolve for the future. There is also the desire to do homage to a law which we have broken or an ideal which we have flouted, and to make plain to ourselves if to no one else that we are not getting off scot free. There are times when one wishes one could do something really significant and costly, and then it can be a salutary humiliation to accept the token penances which are commonly imposed upon us. For the truth is that no penance which we are able to perform can be remotely adequate to the occasion which calls it forth, and this too is a lesson which we have to learn.

Here then is the new face of the problem as our analysis presents it. We cannot be saved without full repentance, and even an imperfect repentance brings with it at least the desire to do worthy penance. But the sickness from which we suffer is that of a diseased will, and so we cannot perform this full repentance nor the penance which should go with it. Yet on the other hand, as we have seen, no one, not even Christ, can do these things for us, if by 'for' is meant 'instead of' us. To this problem there is only one solution. Since we cannot do it alone and He cannot do it instead of us, it must be both together who do it, He in us and we in Him. And in saying this we have stepped out of that whole region of substitutions, contracts and external relationships in which the argument of this lecture has hitherto moved. We have come back at last to that which was missing in the theory under discussion. We find our salvation after all in our mystical union with Christ.

It remains to show in detail how this union makes possible the solution of the problem which was insoluble without it.

The whole life, passion and death of Christ is a sacrifice to the Father, at least in the sense that it is an act of homage, an act of obedience and worship. But how is it also a sacrifice 'for sin'? It is so because it cancels sin. It does not merely cancel the consequences of sin, it does not merely free us from the penalty, it frees us from the sin itself, cleansing us, in Toplady's words, from its guilt and power. It does this precisely because 'Jesus Christ who died at Jerusalem' is also Christ present in the soul by the Spirit, purging, transforming, refashioning us in His own likeness, so that in His obedience we return to obedience and in His worship we worship the Father.

His sacrifice, when we are thus drawn into it and made partakers in it, expiates our offence by destroying in us the root from which it sprang, so that we are no longer the rebellious beings that we were, but a new creation in Christ. It propitiates the Father by bringing us before Him as His true children, accepted in the Beloved.

The theory which we have been discussing drew a picture of Christ, at once priest and victim, appearing before the Father 'on our behalf'. So much is scriptural. But it also interpreted 'on our behalf' as meaning 'instead of us'; Christ offers instead of us the oblation which we cannot make, He pays instead of us the debt of worship and of expiation which we cannot pay. In the light of what has been said about our mystical union with Christ, this substitution doctrine cannot survive without serious modification, for it turns out that the things which Christ is said by this doctrine to do on our behalf are things which we also do in Him. Christ appears before the Father, and we appear in Him; Christ has made the perfect offering, and we as His members join in the making of it; Christ is seated on the Throne and we are seated there with Him.

Christian devotion will never cease to say that Christ in His Passion 'paid the price' of sin. The truth of this phrase is not in question, but what does it really mean? It means that He accepted the consequences of sin, that He did and underwent what was necessary as a result of it. The toil and pain are the 'price of sin' in the sense that they are what has to be undergone when sin has been yielded to. Again, since the toil and pain are the necessary consequences of sin, they can also be referred to as its 'penalty' – the only kind of penalty, as we saw, which God inflicts; and so Christ in undergoing the consequences of sin can also be said to 'pay the penalty' of it. Yet this is true only in an elliptical sense, and is open to misconstruction. Strictly speaking, Christ undergoes that which is in fact the penalty of sin: but He does not undergo it as a penalty, for He has incurred none, and He does not undergo it instead of us, but for us and with us. As early as Origen and again in Athanasius the point is emphasised that Christ underwent death, which is the penalty of our sin, not in order that we might not die but in order that we might die aright. Our death without Him would be punishment and sheer destruction; with Him and in Him it is saving penance and redemptive sacrifice.

'Penance' suggests 'penitence', and so opens up another aspect of the matter. It is a point frequently made in discussions on the Passion, and based ultimately on a biblical utterance, that Christ on the Cross 'condemned' sin once for all. He condemned it in at least two senses. The process of events which brought Him to the Cross shows the nature of sin in all its loathsomeness with a clarity not to be surpassed. But more than this. The life of Christ on earth was a continual and successful battle against temptation. He met the full impact of sin in its attractiveness as well as in its terror, and unwaveringly rejected it. His acceptance of the Cross seals that rejection once for all; sin after this can neither attract nor terrorise any more and in so far as we are in Him, His rejection of sin becomes also ours. This is our true penitence, which, like all good things, is in us only as His gift. And thus we can sift the true from the false in Moberly's bold theory of Christ Himself as the only perfect penitent. Only the sinless, says Moberly, can be perfectly penitent for sin. The sinner himself cannot do it, but the perfect penitence of the innocent makes up what is wanting in the imperfect penitence of the guilty. Taken literally this is more than a paradox, it is a psychological impossibility. Repentance is something which Christ cannot possibly perform in our stead. One cannot, properly speaking, even if one is God, repent of what one has not done. But that which in Christ is a perfect rejection of sin *ab initio* becomes in us, His members, a penitence for sin which grows as we grow nearer to Him.

Is there then nothing which Christ can be said to do instead of us? Is there nothing to justify the substitutionary language

which is so deeply woven into Christian devotion? Indeed
there is, and we see it at two points.

Firstly, in the whole process of our redemption it is He who
takes the initiative and retains it throughout. He alone meets
the full force of the enemy's power and He alone wins the
decisive victory. None of us could bear the full impact of evil
nor the full weight of the suffering which redeems. We have
not the power and we have not the will to do it. Christ
awakens the will in us and gives us the power, so far as we are
in Him, yet never in a perfect degree. To each is given that
share of the struggle and of the Cross which he is able to bear.
On Christ alone the full weight of evil broke, He alone bore
the full burden, He alone won a victory which was self-
wrought and all-decisive. 'I looked, and there was none to
help, and I wondered that there was none to uphold; therefore
mine own arm brought salvation unto me, and my fury, it
upheld me.'[1]

Secondly, to be in Christ is to be a new creature, different
from that which one was before and different from what one
could ever be in oneself. It is this new creature, this new self,
not the old and sinful one, which finds acceptance before God.
We are acceptable to God because what He sees in us is not
ourselves, but Christ; or (to put it another way) we are acceptable because He sees us not as we are in ourselves, but as we
are in Christ. 'Not I, but Christ in me.' 'Not in myself, but
in Christ.' This is the true substitution, which the theories
mishandle and misconceive, but which the Bible and the
Church proclaim and on which Christian devotion continually
dwells. Analysis discloses it in the often-used image of the
blood of Christ, whether this is conceived as the protective
blood of the Paschal Lamb, or as the sanctifying blood of the
covenant-victim, or as the inebriating chalice of the eucharist,
or however else the image of the precious blood may be set
forth; for to receive the blood in any of these ways, to be

[1] Isaiah 63.5.

smeared or sprinkled with it or to drink it or however else it may be applied, is to become identified with a life which is not one's own and to draw safety and fresh vigour from that identification. But the clearest statement of the relationship is to be found in the well-known lines:

> *Look, Father, look on His anointed face,*
> *And only look on us as found in Him.*

These words occur in an eucharistic hymn, and this, I would suggest, is no accident. In the Catholic world, whose worship has revolved about the eucharist, the unbalanced theories which I have been criticising have often been accepted and taught, but their effect has always been offset by the presence of a richer and truer theology embodied in the liturgy. It is in those parts of Christendom where the eucharist has been neglected, or where a minimising doctrine of it has prevailed, that the doctrine of the Atonement too has taken on a meagre and ill-proportioned and often misleading form.

IV

Justification

IT IS paradoxical that we should have got so far without examining the doctrine of justification, which plays such a central part in discussions of the Atonement wherever the influence of the Reformation has been felt. The doctrine of justification by faith alone is one of the central doctrines of Reformation theology. It is drawn from the writings of St. Paul, who expounds it with vigour and with tolerable clarity. True, in his writings it has not that central place which it has in Reformation doctrine, and in the rest of the New Testament, though the doctrine is nowhere contradicted (except in a purely verbal way by St. James), it is nowhere preached with Pauline emphasis and clarity, while in pre-Reformation theology it plays a somewhat undistinguished part. It is the Reformation which has placed it and kept it in the centre of theological debate, and while doing so has also raised controversy about its meaning.

The phrase 'justification by faith' raises two problems, or rather sets of problems, those relating to justification and those relating to faith. In this chapter I shall confine myself to the problems relating to justification. Faith will furnish a theme for another lecture. One need only consult the standard textbooks of theology, Catholic and Protestant, to see that the word is used in quite different senses by these two groups. It is with this duality of meaning that we must begin, and seek to clear it up by examining the word itself and also its historical and literary background.

The verb 'to justify' belongs to a family of English verbs

which are formed by adding to an adjective the suffix '-ify'. There is a corresponding family of verbs in Latin and again in Greek; in Hebrew the *hiphil* form of the verb furnishes a rough equivalent. In all these languages the primary and obvious meaning of the words or word-forms in question is to confer an attribute on something. To clarify is to make clear, to purify is to make pure, to sanctify is to make sacred or holy; and so by analogy to justify should be to make just. There are however instances of such words bearing a different shade of meaning from this. In modern English, for example, to verify is not always or most frequently to make true; it is more commonly to check whether something is true, or to show that it is so. If I say that it is raining and it actually is, the rain which is falling may be said to verify my statement in that it makes it true, but it is the sight of the rain which I get when I look out of the window which verifies my statement in the sense of showing it to be true. With the word 'justify' the case is even more complex. In strict etymology, to justify a man should be to make him just, to make him a man of righteous habits and character, but in ordinary English usage the word never means this. In ordinary usage 'justification' relates not to a man's character and personality but to his overt actions. A man performs an action the rightness of which is called in question. To justify the action means to show that it was right, and this is done by pointing to the circumstances and considerations which justify the action in the sense of making it right. The man himself is said to be justified in doing something when his action is itself justified, i.e. when the circumstances are such as to make it the right action. The man can 'justify himself' by showing that this is the case.

So much for English. The corresponding types of words in Latin, Greek and Hebrew are beset with similar though not identical ambiguities, and this is true in particular of the words corresponding to our word 'justify'.

When St. Paul speaks of justification he is usually thinking of man on trial before God his judge, who, as the Bible frequently says, judges men according to their works. Man is then called upon to justify himself (i.e. show that he has acted rightly) by pointing to facts and considerations which justify what he has done (i.e. make it right). So at least we should say in modern English. But this cannot be what St. Paul has in mind when he speaks of justification. For that which makes a man's actions right or just is the purpose with which and the circumstances in which they are performed; that which proves a man or his actions just is an argument advanced by the man himself or by someone speaking on his behalf. But in St. Paul it is God who justifies, and it is God in His capacity as judge, not as counsel for the defence. In that context, to justify can only mean 'to pronounce just', and for the judge to pronounce the prisoner just or righteous is in fact to acquit him. In St. Paul's standard doctrine this is undoubtedly what the word means. The justification of the sinner is his acquittal at God's bar.

Does it mean only this? If we look at the use of the verb *dikaioun* in classical Greek and in the LXX we shall be inclined to say yes. Both in classical Greek and in the LXX *dikaiousthai* means to have justice done to one or to have a judicial sentence pronounced upon one, and it means nothing else. In particular it never means to be rendered just or righteous, any more than 'justification' means that in modern English. And yet in Christian theology from the time of the Fathers onwards, with the sole exception of the Protestant world, the word has constantly had this latter meaning. Has it this meaning in St. Paul, in addition to the meaning of acquittal? Does St. Paul use the word in two senses? And, whether he does so or not, is it in fact true to say that we are justified in both senses, that we are both acquitted and made righteous?

Let us begin by examining the conception of justice or righteousness itself and its background in social history.

All human societies care for righteousness among their

members, and all human societies before this present century seem to have found a source and sanction for this righteousness in their gods. What is this 'righteousness' which they seek? It is more than mere distributive justice, or fair dealing in matters of exchange. Plato's definition of *dikaiosyne* comes fairly close to it. A man is righteous (*ṣaddiq, dikaios*) if he is and does what is appropriate in his station and in his relations with other people. This formula holds good for all men, but in the special case where the man is a king it leads to an interesting consequence. A king is righteous, i.e. does what is required of him in his position as king, if he ensures that his subjects all do what is required of them in their own several positions. Thus a king's righteousness is not merely a matter of his private conduct; it involves the active promotion of righteousness among his people, which of course he may do in various ways, by judgment, by precept, by example, and so on. This is even more true of a god, who is indeed the real and ultimate king, of whom the earthly king is only the deputy. The god shows his righteousness by maintaining and even creating righteousness among his people: he punishes the wicked, vindicates the oppressed, and makes known his righteous law.

The Bible accepts this view of the relation between God and His people. And from this it follows that God's way with sinners can be no simple and obvious way. For the sinner purely as such, the man who has offended against God's righteous law and 'corrupted his way', deserves nothing but condemnation and chastisement. But on the other hand he is only a sinner because he has yielded to Satan's advances and fallen under his power; and from this point of view God's righteousness should surely show itself in delivering him from that tyranny. Surely, too, God will make known His righteousness most effectively not by destroying the offender, but by converting him and writing His righteous law in his heart. So interpreted, God's 'righteousness' becomes equivalent to His 'salvation', and it is thus that the Bible constantly regards it.

The Bible promises that God will do all these things: chastise the guilty, deliver the oppressed, and make His people righteous. But how does this work out in real life? Who that knows himself can presume to rank himself among the righteous? Who can delude himself that God's law is truly written on his own heart? Who can refuse to make the Psalmist's prayer his own?

> 'Enter not into judgment with Thy servant,
> For no man living is righteous before Thee.'[1]

There is indeed another psalm which appears to find an argument of hope in the very fact of the universality of sin:

> 'If Thou, 'Yah,' wilt mark iniquities,
> O Lord, who shall stand?
> But with Thee is forgiveness,
> That Thou mayest be feared.'[2]

Non-Christian Jewish theology has generally tended to rest at this point, admitting the fact of sin but confiding in God's sovereign mercy, which will not allow man's perversity to defeat it. But is this really a solution and not rather a fresh statement of the problem? God's eyes are too pure to look upon iniquity but that does not mean that He can simply overlook it. He is pledged, in fact, to destroy it. But the Old Testament does not tell us how God can destroy sin without destroying us with it, nor how our relations with Him can be made tolerable when the evil in us has so obviously not yet been rooted out.

It is St. Paul's intense concern with this problem which has shaped Christian thought on the subject. Modern Jewish commentators point to this as a decisive cleavage between Judaism and Christianity. This, they say, is something which Paul never learned from Gamaliel, and they ascribe it to some morbid streak in his character. It is in fact not Judaistic, but it

---

[1] Psalm 143.2.   [2] Psalm 130.3.

is not therefore merely morbid. It is Christian, and it is a necessary consequence of the seriousness with which the Gospels insist on the divine law of perfection. St. Paul was wiser than those recent Christians who have imagined that the Sermon on the Mount was part of the gospel. It is not the gospel, it is the Law, with whose oppressive and intolerable perfection only the gospel can enable us to live. The gospel, by contrast, is the news of forgiveness and renewal, a forgiveness which we can never earn and a renewal or return to righteousness which we can never by ourselves achieve. It is from start to finish a free gift of God to the undeserving, and that is why St. Paul, who starts with the profoundest pessimism, ends with songs of triumph and gratitude.

I have said that the good news is news of forgiveness and also of renewal or return to righteousness. The relation between these two aspects of it must be considered carefully, for in this relation lies a great part of the Reformation controversy. We must consider it as it is in fact; as it is reflected in biblical and later terminology; and as it works itself out in religious experience and discipline.

I. JUSTIFICATION AS FORGIVENESS AND ACCEPTANCE IN CHRIST

Forgiveness is the main aspect of justification as it is presented in the argument of Romans. The epistle begins with the fact that no man is righteous before God. No man can escape from God now or hereafter, and no one can come before Him otherwise than as a sinner. That, it seems, must mean that everyone stands condemned. But for one who is in Christ this is not so. To be in Christ is to stand before the Father in the Son, and when a man so stands, the Father sees in him not the sinner that he has been and is, but the member of Christ that he is and is to be. On that footing a man can be accepted, regarded with favour, admitted to the divine fellowship, even while he is still infected with sin, and thus, in St. Paul's language 'the sinner is justified'.

We cannot understand this except in the light of that paradox which runs through the whole New Testament doctrine of the Christian life. We are and we are not what we appear to be. What we have been and still are is dead to us and we to it. We are already in faith and hope what we are to be, and not only do our own faith and hope present us in this light, but God Himself sees us thus. The paradox is forced upon us as we read what St. Paul has to say about the Church, the greatness and majesty and holiness of the Church appearing side by side with and in no way diminished by the scandals in the Church's actual life. The Church is dwelling in the heavenly places at the very same time that its members are fuddled with drink and fornication, for all that is of the earth, though it continues in time, is already dead in the eyes of God, and our real life is hid with Christ in Him. What is true of the Church is true also of the individual Christian. To be in Christ does not mean an immediate end of sinning, but it does mean immediate deliverance from the status of a sinner, from guilt and condemnation. We are not really what we are of ourselves, but what we are in Christ, and His righteousness 'covers' our iniquity. The Christian devotion of later days has fastened upon this Hebrew image of expiation as the covering of guilt:

> *Plenteous grace with Thee is found,*
> *Grace to cover all my sin.*

An equivalent image is that of the righteousness of Christ as the new robe in which the sinner is clad:

> *Jesu, Thy blood and righteousness*
> *My beauty are, my glorious dress.*

There is a way of thinking about man's status before God which treats it as something to be settled hereafter, at the Last Day or at the particular judgment after death. As the judgment is future, so is the verdict, and in this life one cannot know for certain what the verdict will be. One can only hope for acquittal, and trust to be forgiven. Phrases of this kind used to have a fairly wide currency among Christians, and even today there are many people who think of the Christian doctrine of salvation in these terms. St. Paul has nothing to do with such a post-dated forgiveness. The Pauline Christian does not hope to be forgiven, he knows himself forgiven here and now. The charge-sheet that had been drawn up against him has been cancelled, the favourable verdict has been pronounced. 'There is now no condemnation for those who are in Christ Jesus.' And he who stands in God's forgiveness can also hold up his head before men. 'Who shall lay anything to the charge of God's elect? It is God who justifies; who is he that shall condemn?'

Nor is the gift of justification confined to the cancelling of the charge-sheet and the release of the prisoner. Justification is far more than mere acquittal and remission of penalty. The discharged prisoner is drawn back, nay, welcomed back, into the life of the family of God. He lives not merely in God's forgiveness but in His favour. No longer tongue-tied in conscious guilt, set free from fear and crippling shame, he addresses God as 'Father' and enjoys what St. John calls 'freedom of speech' in His presence. The useless slave (*doulos achreios*, Luke 17.10) is set free by the son of the house (John 8.36) and promoted to the status of a friend (John 15.15). With peace of mind and healthy confidence he is set free to live, not in his own strength but in the power of the Spirit, that life of obedience and fellowship for which he was created and which is his eternal joy.

This body of doctrine, though clearly present in the New Testament, had not before the Reformation that central place in theological discussion which the Reformers gave to it. Why did they do this? What was the problem, in their minds fundamental, to which this doctrine offered the solution? It was the problem of the fear of judgment, the sense of insecurity which results from living under the shadow of an impending doom with no clear assurance of safety.

There is of course a sense in which this fear is fundamental to the Christian life. The fear of the Lord is the beginning of wisdom. It spurs us on when hope and love are too weak to do so, and no one who is not yet perfected in love can do without it. But a foundation should support its superstructure without obtruding itself or dominating the whole edifice, and there have been times in Christian history when the fear of judgment has dominated and overshadowed the spiritual life of many people. It has always been characteristic of popular Christianity to let the moral overshadow the mystical, and to conceive the moral life itself in terms of law rather than of love. One can say this without forgetting the richness and vigour of the mystical life in the Church; for after all the Christianity of the ordinary man and the preaching and teaching which he has received have not normally been of a mystical stamp. The Christianity of the common man has too often been one in which God appears mainly as creator and judge, and in which man's chief concern is to ensure a favourable verdict in the judgment. Christianity is the divine law. Christ is the revealer of the new law which fulfils and supersedes the old and Christ again is the judge of quick and dead. The fact that he is also our advocate, and the reason why He can be so, *viz.* our mystical union with Him, is largely forgotten. Instead we are supposed to work our way to heaven by fulfilling God's commandments and so accumulating merit; and the guilt of sin is to be offset or expiated by penitential observances, supported by the intercessions of the saints.

Such at any rate was the version of Christianity which the Reformers found current among many of their contemporaries, and they rightly regarded it as a perversion of the faith. The point of the doctrine of justification, as they understood it and preached it, was that God's forgiveness and favour cannot be earned, and that any attempt to earn them is wholly misguided,

but that they are to be received, and that everyone can receive
them, here and now as a free gift in Christ. This lifts from
men's shoulders the burden of an intolerable anxiety. It turns
Christianity back again from being merely a new Law into
being a gospel. It proclaims freedom and bestows confidence,
and this without waiting for the sinner to rid himself of his sin.
Precisely here, in the paradox that it is the sinner who is justified, lies the glad news as the Reformation saw it. Hence those
pregnant phrases which echo down in the Protestant tradition.
Pecca fortiter, says Luther; he does not mean 'let yourself go
and do not worry', but 'be bold in God's forgiveness in spite
of the sin which still clings about you'. Again we hear of
justificatio impii, and we are told that the Christian is *simul justus
et peccator*. All these phrases mean the same thing. It is true, for
it is Pauline, but it owes its special importance in Reformation
teaching to the emotional tension from which the Reformation
was born.

2. IMPUTED OR IMPARTED RIGHTEOUSNESS?

Simul justus et peccator. What does the word *justus* mean in
this phrase? Its primary meaning is not in doubt: it refers to
the Christian's status, and means that he is reckoned as just by
God's merciful verdict in spite of all the unrighteousness that
is in him. But can it mean – does it mean – should it mean
something else as well? Should it be taken as referring to the
real state or character of the Christian? Is God content, while
pronouncing the sinner righteous, to leave him in his actual
unrighteousness? Or does He, while accepting him as righteous
in Christ, at the same time set about making him really so? Is
the righteousness of the Christian a merely imputed righteousness, or is it also an imparted one?

Everything that I have said so far in these lectures compels
the answer: imparted. Surely this is obvious. The theory of
a merely imputed righteousness goes most easily with a vicari-

ous expiation theory of the kind which I criticised in my last lecture. In common Protestant teaching it has in fact very often been associated with such a theory. Then the doctrine runs thus: I myself am not righteous at all, but Christ's righteousness is accepted instead of mine in payment of the debt which I owe to the Father. The records of Protestant preaching and Protestant devotion abound in examples of this way of talking. But we have already seen that legal arrangements and legal fictions of this sort are not to be ascribed to God. We have already seen that the true formula of salvation is not 'Christ instead of me' but 'Christ in me and I in Him'; and if we say this the theory of a merely imputed righteousness at once becomes incredible. How can I be in Christ, who is all righteousness, and not myself be made righteous? What can be meant by being in Him if not that His life is communicated or imparted to me? And how can I receive His life without also receiving the character of that life?

It is true that no righteousness of my achieving can ever be a ground for God's approval. All that is of me and from me is thoroughly tainted. The righteousness of God, made mine in hope and increasingly mine in fact through Christ, is mine only as His gift, and in this life I open myself to receive it only imperfectly. There is thus an element of anticipation in everything that is said about the Christian while still in this life; we are now in hope, i.e. in expectation, what we shall be afterwards in actuality. But still the difference between the then and the now is not a difference between being and not being; it is the difference between the full-grown plant and the quickening seed, between the mature and the inchoate. What we shall one day fully be, that we are already in part. God's judgment in counting us righteous is therefore never wholly false in fact (how could it be?), there is never a moment when we have been pronounced righteous but have not yet begun to be made so. Acquittal and restoration, forgiveness and the beginning of the new life go together. God sees in us what we are and are to be. This is in accord with the Old Testament principle that the Word of God is a creative Word. If God calls us righteous, He at the same time makes us so; in Charles Wesley's words, He 'speaks our souls restored'.

Here then is the true righteousness of the Christian, and the relation between it and God's merciful judgment upon him. God does not pronounce us righteous because of ourselves we are so, but neither does He pronounce us righteous without Himself making us so in Christ. Is this biblical doctrine? Undoubtedly it is. Is it part of what St. Paul means by the word 'justification'? That is a more difficult question, but here again I believe that the answer is yes.

It is certainly part of his teaching about the Christian life. He and St. John are our principal sources for a detailed doctrine on this subject, and they are both emphatic in presenting it as a changed life. It is a new birth, a resurrection from the dead, a translation from earth to heaven, a new creation. On the face of it, these tremendous images are meant to convey not only a reconciliation but also a transformation. That this is their meaning becomes certain when we consider the wealth of teaching which St. Paul gives us about the Christian virtues, the imitation of Christ, the gifts and fruits of the Spirit. Most people would agree that a great part, if not the whole, of what he says under these heads amounts to a description of a new and distinctively Christian type of 'righteousness'. He uses the word himself in the well-known passage in Ephesians 6.14, where he bids us put on the breastplate of righteousness along with the rest of the Christian panoply. *Dikaiosyne* here could at a pinch be taken to mean the Christian's justified status, and the 'wiles' and 'fiery darts' of the evil one could be doubts as to one's salvation, which faith and the gospel and the consciousness of justification through Christ will help to ward off. If St. Paul were a seventeenth-century Calvinist persecuted by Satan with doubts of his election, this interpretation would be reasonable and the whole paragraph could be read in that sense.

But St. Paul is a first-century Jew with a strong ethical sense, and in the previous paragraphs he has been giving advice about conduct. He has even spoken in verse 8 about 'doing good' and 'receiving a return' for it. The natural and obvious sense of the passage is therefore that we are to be righteous, to cultivate and strengthen our righteousness.

What then of St. Paul's use of the verb 'to justify'? Does this mean to make righteous as well as to acquit? Here I think we must go carefully. In the Epistles to the Romans and Galatians St. Paul is writing controversially, working out an argument which is directed towards a particular point, and does not necessarily say all that is in his mind. He is discussing the position of man before his judge, and arguing that if man is to be acquitted in the judgment it must be by free grace, since man cannot earn his acquittal. Man cannot win favour by being righteous, he can only obtain favour by being accounted righteous. In this context, to be justified must mean primarily to be reckoned as righteous, and the 'overt logic' (as Moberly called it) of the argument does not require it to have any other meaning. On the other hand it does not exclude the other possible meaning. After saying that we cannot earn God's favour by making ourselves righteous, St. Paul can perfectly well go on to say, if he wishes, that God makes us righteous when He receives us into His favour. As we have seen, that is the truth of the matter and St. Paul knows it.

To me it seems that, as the argument of Romans unfolds, this second meaning of the word 'justification' does begin to shine through. There is more than a hint of it in chapter 5 when St. Paul introduces his parallel between the first and the second Adam. 'So then, as through the transgression of one condemnation spread to all men, so also, through the righteous act (*dikaioma*) of one, justification (*dikaiosis*) and life spread to all men; for as through the disobedience of the one the many were constituted sinners, so also through the obedience of the one the many shall be constituted righteous (*dikaioi*).' The natural interpretation of this is that the real righteousness of Christ is really communicated to those who are His. *Dikaiosis* in verse 18 may well mean imputation of righteousness, since it stands in antithesis with 'condemnation', but 'sinners' and 'righteous' in verse 19 seem naturally to invite the other interpretation. Again, a comparison of 4.25 with 6.4 strongly suggests that justification (*dikaiosis*) is equivalent to newness of life, and the context in chapter 6 shows pretty clearly that this 'newness of life' means a real repudiation of sin and a real liberation from it, not only from its guilt but from its power (6.14, whose meaning is fixed by comparison with 7.11). In a word, St. Paul in Romans says more than the 'overt logic' of his argument requires him to say. He is not satisfied to say what will refute the Jewish legalist and leave the matter there. He goes on to describe the fullness of God's unspeakable gift. In chapters 7 and 8 the original argument has been swallowed up into something far greater – a hymn of the risen life in Christ. The word 'justification' grows with the growth of the theme, and ends by meaning nothing less than the risen life itself.

3. THE VERBAL DISPUTE AND WHAT LIES BEHIND IT

There is thus good reason to think that when pre-Reformation writers speak of justification as the being made righteous, they are speaking in accordance with one part though not with the whole of St. Paul's mind. The same may be said of the definitions of the Council of Trent. These however will repay further examination, both in themselves and in relation to the Protestant declarations against which they were directed or which were renewed in reply to them. For on the Protestant side we find a determined attempt to tie down 'justification' to 'acquittal' and to deny that it means anything else at all.

In the Tridentine *Decree on Justification*, chapter vii, we find the following words: 'Justification ... is not only the remission of sins, but also the sanctification and renewal of the inner man ... whereby a man, from unrighteous, is made righteous, and from an enemy a friend. ... We are renewed in the spirit of our mind, and are not merely accounted righteous, but are truly called so and are so. ... This ... comes about when ... by the Holy Ghost the love of God is shed abroad in the hearts of those who are justified and inheres in them, so that in justification itself, along with the remission of sins, a man has all these things simultaneously infused into him through Jesus Christ, into whom he is grafted, *viz.* faith, hope and charity.'

If my argument so far has been sound, this is a true account of justification. It clearly states that the 'remission of sins' is part of the meaning of the word, but it says that the 'infusion' of righteousness is also part of it. This is both correct in itself and true to the mind of St. Paul. It does not stress the remission side of the matter as strongly as St. Paul does, partly because it was written as a counterblast to the Protestant teaching which dwelt upon that side to the exclusion of the other, and partly because its interest is only dogmatic whereas St. Paul's, like that of the Protestants, is largely experiential. For these reasons it is not a perfectly balanced summary of what he says in Romans and Galatians though it is better balanced than the Protestant interpretation of those epistles. It teaches no error and it denies a serious error, and in sum it is a valuable safeguard of the integrity of the faith.

One difficulty which I do feel about it I will state here only in the form of a question. The words of this decree identify justification in its more positive sense, as the renewal of life, with sanctification. Is this really correct? Is there really no difference between righteousness and holiness? Inseparable they may be from one another, as they both are from the forgiveness of sins, but that alone does not justify us in treating them as identical in essence. In my second lecture I tried to exhibit them as distinct. Was I mistaken in doing so? If not,

74

it will follow that Trent, though right in the substance of what it says, is guilty of a certain confusion of terms.

I will say no more about Trent, but about the Reformers there is much to be said. They could not but be aware that it lies in God's purpose not merely to grant us remission of sins, but to bestow upon us the gift of a new life. The pages of St. Paul about the virtues and the gifts and the life in the Spirit were open to them as to everyone else. They knew that we are not merely to be received into favour, but to grow in grace. But whereas Trent gives to this life of grace the double name of justification and sanctification, the Reformers call it sanctification only, and make justification mean only forgiveness. They add that justification and sanctification so understood, though distinct, are never found apart.

'Since faith receives Christ as He is offered by the Father, and He is offered not only for righteousness, forgiveness of sins and peace, but also for sanctification, as a fountain of living waters, it is certain that faith cannot recognise Him rightly without receiving the sanctification of His Spirit.' These are Calvin's words, in which the meanings of the terms are clearly delimited. Parallels could be found in Luther and in other Reformation writers. But the clearest statement of the distinction between justification and sanctification in this Protestant sense of justification is perhaps to be found in John Wesley's sermon on Justification by Faith. 'But what is it to be justified? What is justification? . . . It is evident . . . that it is not the being made actually just and righteous. This is sanctification, which is indeed in some degree the immediate fruit of justification, but nevertheless is a distinct gift of God and of a totally different nature. The one implies what God does for us through His Son, the other what He works in us by His Spirit.' In these pronouncements two things leap to the eye. First, they confine justification to acquittal, and in this I have already argued that Trent is right as against them. And consequently they are compelled to agree

75

with Trent in identifying the life of grace with sanctification, as if there were no difference between being righteous and being holy.

Why do the Protestants limit justification in this way? It is strange that they should do so, for it is a departure from the plain and natural interpretation of St. Paul. Once more we must explain what they do by reference to their special pre-occupations. We must remember that their main concern in dealing with these matters is not to show us what the Christian is or can become, but to tell us on what ground he is forgiven and accepted by God. To speak of the Christian as 'righteous' in that context is (they think) to incur the risk, or rather the certainty, of suggesting that he is accepted because, having achieved righteousness, he deserves to be accepted; whereas in truth his righteousness while in this life is always inadequate, and in any case is not his own achievement, but the work of the Spirit in him, in and after his initial justification. His righteousness of life and his acceptance before God are not cause and effect, but joint consequences of his incorporation into Christ. It must be admitted that these are important truths, and perhaps there was special need of the emphasis which the Reformers laid upon them in their day and generation. But was it really necessary to enforce them by distorting the language of the Bible?

In strict logic the same arguments which led them to deal thus with 'justification' would apply also to the word 'sanctification'. One might expect to find them interpreting this word on the same principle as its fellow; one might expect them to equate 'holy' with 'sacred' or 'consecrated', and to say that the Christian's 'holiness' lies not in his spiritual state or character, but in his status as one whom God has made His own. That is in fact part of the meaning of the word, though it is not nearly the whole. And it is to be noted that in classical Protestantism, as distinct from various movements of Pietist or Methodist inspiration, the doctrine of personal holiness or sanctification

76

of character, though formally maintained, has been persistently played down. This is consonant with the fact that the Protestants have deliberately broken with the Catholic tradition of ascetic theology and the Catholic discipline of the spiritual life. They are suspicious of any doctrine relating to 'perfection' (although the word is biblical), of any attempt to single out particular persons in the Church as 'saints', and of anything which they think savours of 'mysticism'. Here and there one finds one of them writing as if the coming of Christ and of the Spirit had made no difference at all to the present state of the world or even of the faithful, but only to their standing in the light of God's final judgment.

For all this there is one simple cause – the fear of anything which may seem to obscure the gratuitous and unmerited character of our redemption. Luther put it in a nutshell when he said that in relation to God we are always in the position of beggars. The desire to safeguard this doctrine is the reason why strict Protestants have made such heavy weather about good works, the cultivation of the virtues and the like. To a Catholic these are no problem, because he looks at them from a different point of view. To him the remission of sins is not a standing problem or a theme for anxious thought; for he knows himself baptised and absolved. He is thinking rather how he may grow in grace, and the answer to that question will naturally include various forms of effort and discipline, together with a certain attitude towards those who have gone ahead of him on the way. But the strict Protestant is thinking all the time about forgiveness and reconciliation, and to him virtues and good works and systems of discipline are grounds on which foolish men vainly try to earn their reconciliation. His first concern is to tell us that we cannot earn it, that the remission of sins is a free gift which we can only accept in faith, and he is so anxious to insist that forgiveness cannot be earned that he is suspicious of anyone who points out the complementary truth, that when we are forgiven we are meant to work out our salvation, to grow in holiness and righteousness, by the help of sanctifying grace.

4. JUSTIFICATION IN CHRISTIAN EXPERIENCE

The Reformers' use of the doctrine of justification was rooted in experience. To them the doctrine was important not merely because it happened to be true, but because the knowledge of it solved what was for them the central problem of the spiritual life. Hence came their profound sense of affinity with St. Paul, because he too had found in this doctrine the solution of a similar problem. This psychological aspect of the matter was largely neglected in Christian literature between his time and the Reformation; but this more than anything else may be said to condition the Protestant teaching on the subject, and we may profit by looking at it more closely.

Man is guilty, and he knows he is. Man stands under condemnation, and knows himself condemned. It is the knowledge of one's guilt, the knowledge that one stands in the wrath of God, which creates the psychological problem. To one who knows that he stands in the wrath of God, the thought of God can only be terrible. His impulse will be to escape into forgetfulness or else to raise the persistent cry of Bunyan's Pilgrim, 'What shall I do to be saved?' Nothing can solve his problem which does not remove the burden of anxiety by substituting for the angry judge the figure of the merciful father, and when this substitution is made, man's attitude to God is wholly changed. For insecurity he now has confidence, for fear he now has trust. Before he was tongue-tied in God's presence; now with freedom of access he speaks boldly. This feature of the Christian life is well recognised in the New Testament. 'Freedom of speech' is St. John's word for it, which appears as 'boldness' in the standard English versions.

I have described the atmosphere of anxiety which prevailed among some people in Western Christendom in the years preceding the Reformation. Christianity, which should be a liberation, had instead become a burden; the gospel had been turned into a new Law. The thought of God as the righteous judge stood in the way of the approach to Him as father. From this point of view we can well understand how the Reformers, reading Romans and preaching the doctrine of justification, felt that they were uncovering the original freshness of the gospel. To men who had been taught to try to pile up merit, yet with no hope of ever really having enough, the renewed preaching of the doctrine of God's free grace seemed like a deliverance from Egyptian slavery. In the folk-memory of the Protestant world this picture of it is irremovably lodged.

It is therefore natural that Protestantism should have tended to foster a particular type of spiritual case-history, whose central feature is the initial state of anxiety, followed by a sudden and decisive release. It was the case-history of Luther himself, whose release came when he understood from Romans the true meaning of justification as a free gift. It is the case-history of both the Wesleys, one of whom received the decisive illumination from Luther's commentary on Romans. It is the case-history of untold multitudes in the Protestant world from the beginning until now. This sudden experience of illumination and release is the most typical meaning of the word 'conversion' in Protestant terminology. This is clear both from the direct evidence of Protestant literature and also from the writings of various psychologists who, working mainly with Protestant case-histories, have described under the name of 'conversion' an experience of this type. In the devotional language of Protestantism it is described under a variety of images. In Bunyan it is the removal of the 'burden', i.e. the load of guilt and fear, which falls off of its own accord when Christian passes beneath the Cross. It is the cleansing of the defiled, the healing of the sick or broken-hearted, the release of the captive, the recall of the banished ones. It is the stirring of new life in the spiritually dead, the removal of the heart of stone and the gift of the heart of flesh. It is the assurance (*plerophoria*) of faith and hope, to which Charles Wesley gives expression in a characteristic blending of Pauline and Johannine language:

> *No condemnation now I dread:*
> *Jesus, and all in Him, is mine.*
> *Alive in Him, my living Head,*
> *And clothed with righteousness divine,*
> *Bold I approach the eternal throne,*
> *And claim the crown, through Christ, my own.*

This mighty experience is always connected with the doctrine of justification. But clearly it is not the fact of justification but the consciousness of justification which produces these effects. Much confusion could have been avoided if this distinction between the fact and the consciousness of the fact had always been kept in view. Without it, there is a tendency for what is ostensibly a discussion of justification to turn into a discussion of the consciousness of justification, and for justification itself to be identified with conversion – a mistake which can have unfortunate consequences.

In St. Paul and the other apostolic writers this confusion could hardly arise, for the reason that the Apostles were dealing all the time with people who were converted in adult life. To them the acceptance of the faith, the rites of baptism and confirmation, the gift of justification and the consciousness of release coincided roughly in time, and there was no need to distinguish and analyse as later practice compels us to do. But if we baptise people in infancy when they know nothing about it, and if we also hold that baptism makes the child a member of Christ and therefore necessarily justifies him, we are in the position that every person who has been baptised in infancy remains for a long period justified without knowing it, and needs to be taught to know it. It is possible that through lack of teaching or through defective teaching he may never come to know it, which is a pity; but if in adult life he does come to know it, it is always possible that the knowledge may come as a sudden illumination with striking psychological results such as I have described. Then it may happen, indeed it has too often happened, that the man himself and his spiritual guides imagine that he first became justified at the moment of this experience. There is no hope of clarity in these matters unless we distinguish firmly between justification itself, which is a matter for soteriology, and the consciousness of justification, which is a theme for pastoral and ascetic theology. Once this distinction is drawn, we can go on to recognise the importance of the experience and to ask what part it plays in the unfolding of the spiritual life. This question would have been more satisfactorily answered if the Protestants, who know most about the experience, had had a proper ascetic theology into which to insert it, or if the Catholics, who alone have a proper ascetic theology, could have brought themselves to do something better than to register distaste when the experience is mentioned.

I have discussed this question briefly in an article in *Theology* of May 1945, where I suggest that a study of the symptoms of the conversion experience reveals certain parallels with the earlier stages of the illuminative way. The anxiety and insecurity which precede conversion are not uncharacteristic of the purgative way. The core of the conversion experience itself consists precisely in an illumination which brings with it relief from anxiety, a release of fresh energies, and an increase both in spiritual insight and in power over sin. Experience shows that this is not infrequently followed, though not immediately, by a period of aridity and apparent renewed frustration in which the soul may wonder whether she has not lost what she seemed to have gained. The treatment of this state among Protestants might have been more wisely handled if the experience of the saints with regard to the night of the soul had been understood among them. It is also a weakness in some forms of popular Protestantism that they regard the experience of conversion as the climax of the spiritual life, treating it in practice as an end where in truth it is more nearly a beginning, and leaving the convert wondering what should come next, or trying to live on the memory of a past experience for want of guidance as to the next step. In the wiser forms of Protestantism, and especially in Methodism, there is no hesitation as to what should come next: progressive sanctification, leading towards a state which is clearly meant to be the unitive way. There is room here for careful comparative study which might have irenic consequences. The proper integration of this volcanic experience into the traditional account of the pattern of the spiritual life could only be a gain to all concerned, and would complete the process of clearing up the present confusion of teaching with regard to justification.

V

Saving Faith

JUSTIFICATION, we have said, is a free gift; it comes to us by grace. But St. Paul also says that it results from faith. We are 'justified by faith' (*ek pisteos*), and this phrase and its equivalents occur repeatedly in Romans and in Galatians. The term 'faith' is connected with salvation in another Pauline context, in Colossians 2.12. In this passage there is no mention of justification. Our salvation is described as consisting in dying and rising again in Christ; but this dying and rising again is connected on the one hand with faith and on the other hand with baptism. 'Being buried with Him in baptism, in which we were also raised with Him through faith in the energy of God who raised Him from the dead.' Phrases which are familiar to us from the context of Romans begin to appear in the next two verses: God, we are told, has 'graciously remitted (*charizomenos*) all our transgressions, wiping out the handwriting which stood against us'. The circle is closed if we return to Romans and find there in chapter 4 an account of the nature of faith which contains a reference to the dead being endowed with new life. These four ideas then, God's free grace, faith, baptism, and the raising of the dead, go together in St. Paul's mind. It will be important for the understanding of the nature of faith to consider it in this total context.

The doctrine of justification acquired for the Reformation a greater prominence than it had ever had before, and it brought with it the doctrine of justifying faith. 'Justification by faith' is the most popular of all the slogans of the Reformation. It is a slogan with a negative meaning: it means 'faith and not works', and Luther, as is well known, was so sure of this that he put it into the text of St. Paul where the Apostle himself had not troubled to put it. Not merely *fide* but *sola fide* is the doctrine as he preached it. This doctrine he declared to be the *articulus stantis vel cadentis ecclesiae*. All the Reformers agree with him, and so do their successors to this day. Where this doctrine is preached, they say, there and nowhere else is the true Church.

The Church of England is committed to the doctrine by virtue of Article XI, where we read: 'that we are justified by faith only is a most wholesome doctrine,' and we are referred for further treatment of the subject to one of the Homilies. The Homily in question gives a clear and vigorous presentation of the Reformation doctrine on the point, culminating in these words: 'this faith the Holy Scripture teacheth, this is the strong rock and foundation of Christian religion, this doctrine all old and ancient authors of Christ's Church do approve; this doctrine advanceth and setteth forth the true glory of Christ and beateth down the vain glory of man; this whosoever denieth is not to be counted for a true Christian man, nor for a setter forth of Christ's glory.'

What is this doctrine of justification by faith alone, for which such claims are made? And, in view of the fact that it is based on St. Paul, why has it become such a subject of controversy? For Catholic writers from the Reformation to the present day have denied it and denounced it and declared it to be the root of the Protestant heresy. Was St. Paul then a Protestant? Or are the Protestants mistaken in their interpretation of him? How do the Catholics interpret him? And are they fair in what they say about the Protestants? Here is a many-sided problem of exegesis.

Let us begin by asking what the word *faith* (or *fides*, or *pistis*) means to the ordinary man. There can be little doubt that he thinks of 'faith' primarily as a kind of 'belief' or 'believing'; very naturally, since in the New Testament it is constantly associated with the verb 'to believe' (*credo, pisteuo*). If to have faith is to believe, it seems to follow that faith is belief. We shall find this interpretation deeply entrenched, not only in the mind of the ordinary Christian, but also in Catholic and Protestant theology. But we shall also find it hard to understand how, on this interpretation, faith can be a ground of justification.

The Council of Trent defines faith as a supernatural virtue whereby we believe as true what God has revealed, simply because He has revealed it. A long history of Catholic thinking lies behind this definition. The Catholic mind moves in a region where one can speak of 'the Faith', of true belief and false belief and unbelief, and where faith is thought of in contrast with knowledge or vision. In this context faith of course appears as an intellectual virtue, distinguished from hope and charity as virtues respectively of the affections and of the will. This is a valuable and illuminating conception in its place, but one may doubt whether its place is in a discussion of justification. How can an intellectual gift of the kind in question be a justifying factor? Trent explains that it is so because it is 'the beginning of man's salvation, the ground and root of all justification, without which it is impossible to please God and attain to the fellowship of His children.' Although the Council claims 'the constant consensus of the Catholic Church' in support of this interpretation, one's doubts remain. On this showing faith is a *sine qua non* of justification, but it is no more than that; and it is simply impossible to conceive how St. Paul could have singled it out and thrust it into the foreground as he did if this were all the truth of the matter. The suspicion will not be stifled that the justifying faith of which St. Paul speaks is something more than *fides* in the scholastic and Tridentine sense.

The Reformers on the other hand are primarily concerned with the doctrine of justification, and think of faith first and foremost in that context. But they are so preoccupied with justification in the sense of acquittal, and so determined to make clear that we cannot do anything towards our acquittal, that they too in their own way are led to speak of faith in a manner which distinguishes it sharply from will and action. They too define it as a firm belief or persuasion, or perhaps a kind of knowledge, which is given to us by God, *viz.* the knowledge of His favour towards us. Here are Calvin's words: 'Faith is a firm and sure knowledge of God's good will towards us, founded on the free promise given in Jesus Christ, and revealed to our minds and sealed in our hearts by the Holy Ghost.' Or take this Anglican definition from the second Homily on the Passion: 'Faith, that is to say a sure trust and confidence in the mercies of God, whereby we persuade ourselves that God both hath and will forgive our sins, that He hath accepted us again into His favour, . . . not for our merits or deserts but only and solely for the merits of Christ's death and passion.' To talk of justifying faith in this way really amounts to saying that one is saved by acquiring a confident belief that one is so. We must presume that no reputable theologian, Anglican or other, really meant this, but they only too often succeeded in saying it. Moreover, it is to be feared that some of their followers took them at their word, and that under the name of justification by faith a doctrine of justification by confidence was preached from early times. Trent rightly comes out with the utmost vigour against this doctrine of justification by confidence (*fiducia*). Thus in the twelfth Canon: 'If any shall say that justifying faith is nothing but a confidence in God's mercy which remits sins because of Christ, or that it is by this confidence alone that we are justified, let him be anathema.' One would have difficulty in believing that the vain confidence here anathematised had really been preached by anyone, if the Reformation documents were not there to show that it was.

Yet I believe that behind these unfortunate Protestant definitions there lies something else which they do not adequately express. I believe that we should regard them not as successful attempts to formulate a heresy, but as unsuccessful attempts to declare a truth. To find what that truth was, we must go back behind the Reformers to their source, and examine the doctrine of justifying faith as it is presented by St. Paul. When we do this we are struck at once by the fact that he expounds it in connection with the story of Abraham, making much of a text of Genesis which refers to Abraham, and analysing one of the stories about the Patriarch. The author of Hebrews too, in his great galaxy of the heroes of faith, gives an important place to Abraham. Indeed it is not too much to say that the whole New Testament offers us Abraham as an archetype of Christian faith, and it is to Abraham therefore that we must turn for light upon our problem.

Abraham is a central figure both in the Old Testament and in the New. In the Old Testament he is of course the father of Israel, the recipient of that call to come out of his country and his father's house, from which the whole subsequent history of the Church has flowed. He is the friend of God, from whom God has no secrets, he is the recipient of the promise that in his seed all the nations of the earth shall be blessed. God does not disdain to be known as the God of Abraham. The New Testament begins with the figure of John the Baptist raising the question of what the promises made to Abraham really mean. 'Say not, We have Abraham to our father; for I tell you God is able out of these stones to raise up children for Abraham.' Here is a clear statement that the children of Abraham who inherit the promises are not necessarily his physical descendants. In St. John's gospel we see our Lord emphasising this point. 'They answered and said to Him, "Our father is Abraham." Jesus said to them "If you were children of Abraham you would do the works of Abraham".' The whole Epistle to the Romans is concerned with the question: who are the real children of Abraham, the real Israelites, the heirs of the promise? St. Paul shows explicitly that they are not Abraham's physical descendants but his spiritual children. He is the father of many nations because he is the spiritual father of all those to whom his faith is communicated.

What then is Abrahamic faith? St. Paul refers us to the 15th chapter of Genesis, where Abraham, who is childless, asks God who shall be his heir. He has already received the promise that his seed shall be as the dust of the earth, yet he is still childless and elderly, and his wife is beyond childbearing. In reply to his question he receives no explanation, but the renewed assurance that a child of his loins shall be his heir and that his seed shall be in number as the stars. 'And he believed the Lord and He counted it to him for righteousness.'

What does this mean but that Abraham 'believed' the promises of God, i.e. accepted them as true predictions of what God would do, in face of the long delay and apparent impossibility of their fulfilment? 'He believed in God, who gives life to the dead and calls the things which are not as if they were . . . and without weakening in faith he observed his own body already dead (being about a hundred years old) and the deadness of Sarah's womb, but did not doubt the promise through unbelief but was strengthened in faith, giving glory to God and fully assured that what He has promised He is able to perform. Therefore it was counted to him for righteousness.'

'What then?' we may ask; to believe what God says (if it is really God who says it) is surely a simple and obvious thing to do. Why should this be singled out for special mention in this way? Why should this, rather than any other act, be reckoned to Abraham for righteousness? To understand this we must remember what it was that God said and Abraham believed and we must take the incident in its context in Abraham's life. God made a promise which could not be fulfilled without a miracle. Abraham's acceptance of the promise as true was an act of faith in the supernatural, a belief that God could and would act in him and for him above and beyond his own natural strength, a belief therefore in God as saviour and giver of life. Such a belief must necessarily shape Abraham's relations with

88

God, and through them the course of his whole life. It implies a confident trust in God's providence, and more than that, an unquestioning readiness to do whatever God may require, not merely out of fear or reverence, but in the faith that the command is all of a piece with the promise, that it is all part of God's plan for Abraham. It implies, in short, a complete self-commitment to God, a complete openness and responsiveness to God's guidance, a readiness to receive and become whatever God wills him to receive and become. This attitude is the key to the whole character and career of Abraham as the Old Testament describes it.

In the 15th chapter of Genesis Abraham is shown simply as believing, not as doing anything in consequence of his belief. St. Paul has chosen to quote this incident because it is here that his proof-text about faith being 'reckoned for righteousness' occurs. If however we turn from Romans to Hebrews we shall find the portrait of Abraham drawn more fully, and the active side of it given full emphasis. The Epistle to the Hebrews names Abraham as one of a long list of heroes of faith. It tells how he left his own country at God's summons, not knowing where he was going, dwelt in the promised land without ever possessing it, received through faith the power to beget a son in old age, and then at the command was prepared to kill this son, his only son, the son of promise, 'reckoning that God is able to raise one even from the dead.' This is the story of a man living, as Kierkegaard would say, in the paradox. He is summoned to go out to a new country but is not shown whither; he is promised a multitude of descendants when he has no heir and no apparent chance of getting one; in due course by miracle he receives his son, but is then commanded to offer him in sacrifice; and here the paradox reaches its highest point, for the command contradicts the promise, yet both are from God. At no point does Abraham complain or even doubt. His affairs are in God's hands, not in his own. God says He has a work to do for Abraham and through him. God knows what He intends to do and is able to do it. For Abraham there is nothing but to obey where he can, and for the rest to believe and trust.

It is clear beyond question in Hebrews that faith is thought of as a spring of action. But we need not have gone outside Romans to learn this lesson. In Romans 14 we find a distinction drawn between actions which are, and others which are not, 'of faith' (*ek pisteos*), and 'whatever is not of faith is sin'. The kind of action St. Paul has in mind here is the breaking of a tabu, and to do it 'from faith' is to take to oneself the freedom of a Christian man, quietly and confidently, because one believes that this is God's guidance to one in Christ. Without this motive, St. Paul says, the action cannot be guiltless. Here is the doctrine of justifying faith in a nutshell. On the one hand, faith is no inert belief or emotional state, but a motive which issues in action, and on the other hand it is this motive itself, and nothing else, which justifies the act and the agent.

This then is Abrahamic faith, the faith which was counted to Abraham for righteousness, and is counted to us too for righteousness when we come to possess it – an unquestioning self-commitment to God in trust and obedience. An analogy to it may be seen in the attitude of one who places himself under the care of a doctor or of a psychiatrist. No one does this if he thinks he can cure himself; to place oneself under treatment is to declare that one has despaired of oneself as a healer. The doctor in taking on the case will expect to have full control of what is done; he will expect that no other doctor shall be consulted unless he himself calls one in, and that the patient shall not try any measures of his own in addition to those which the doctor prescribes or approves. In this sense the patient's self-committal to the doctor must be complete and absolute. To some extent the patient will in fact be passive, the doctor will do certain things to him and he will undergo the treatment, but very likely too the doctor will instruct him to do certain things himself, and here in a sense the patient will be active. Yet even here what he does will be done in obedience. The ultimate responsibility for it will not be his, and when the cure is complete it will be true to say that he has been cured by the doctor and not by himself. The doctor took the whole responsibility for devising and directing the treatment, and so deserves the whole credit for the cure. This analogy is particularly apt in view of the regular habit, in biblical and later Christian writers, of treating sin as a disease and the saviour as a healer. The analogy falls short of the reality in that neither the doctor nor even the psychiatrist can act upon his patient otherwise than from without. When the Christian places himself thus unquestioningly in the hands of Christ, he is also united with Christ and made a living member of Him. This of course only emphasises the more how completely the healing process is Christ's own act and not ours in distinction from His.

How then, and in what sense, does such self-commitment justify? In the light of all that has been said this is surely no problem. To have faith is to put oneself unconditionally into Christ's hands, and His response to this act of self-surrender is to make us effectively one with Himself. Scripture tells us plainly enough that faith brings the believer into an intimate and life-giving union with Christ. St. Paul says as much when he prays 'that Christ may dwell in your hearts by faith'. Again, if we compare his saying that 'there is now no condemnation for those who are in Christ Jesus' with St. John's saying that 'he who believes is not judged', it seems to follow that to believe and to be in Christ Jesus are equivalent terms. Again, if we examine closely the 6th chapter of St. John's gospel, comparing for instance the 47th with the 51st verse, it seems to follow that 'to believe' is equivalent to 'eating the bread of life', and the bread of life is Christ Himself. The Anglican liturgy speaks St. John's language therefore when it bids the communicant 'feed on Him in thy heart by faith'.

Now, if I become thus united with Christ and effectively a

member of Him, I cease to that extent to be an independent agent. I shall of course continue to do many things, indeed I shall probably be more active and more effective than I was before, but in the last resort they will not be my own actions even though I perform them. It will be not I, but Christ in me, and this I which is also Christ in me is the only I that counts in the sight of God. Everything in me which resists incorporation into Christ stands under condemnation, and in the course of the treatment will be caused to perish, and I myself condemn it and wish it to perish, though it is Christ who must kill it and not I by myself. The real I is what I am in Christ, and this my true self will grow as the other self dies. And I in Christ stand before the Father clothed in His sonship and glorious in His righteousness, which is imputed to me without reserve, and imparted to me already in some degree, though awaiting the perfect work of grace in order to reach its fullness. Faith, in short, by making me one with Christ, is both the ground of God's merciful judgment which absolves me here and now, and the power behind my growth in actual righteousness which has so far only begun. It justifies me in both senses of the word.

Such is justifying faith as the New Testament leads us to conceive it, and I think that at the heart of Protestantism there has always been an understanding of this. Luther, for example, puts it clearly enough when he draws a distinction between *believing things about God*, as I may believe things about any other thing or person, and *believing in God*, as I do when I 'put my trust in Him, surrender myself to Him and make bold to have dealings with Him, believing without doubt that He will be to me and do to me just what is said of Him'. This is well said. This is true biblical doctrine, and this is what echoes through the language of Protestant devotion when one hears the oft-repeated phrases about faith 'fastening upon the Promises'. The definitions which Trent criticises, and which I have criticised, are not truly representative. They are abstract formulae adopted with a polemical purpose. The real tradition of Protestant devotion, nourished on the Bible, displays true Abrahamic faith of the kind which I have analysed. Modern Protestant writers, in speaking of faith, insist that what is meant is a personal relationship with God in Christ; they use words like 'trust' and 'self-commitment', and would agree with what I have said about Abraham. And Catholic writers, aware of this and trying to express it in their own terminology,[1] have sometimes suggested that what Protestants call 'faith' is really faith (in the narrower scholastic and Tridentine sense) and hope and love all in one.

It is a tempting suggestion, and at first sight a plausible one. After all, St. Paul does link faith very closely with love. He speaks of 'faith energising through love', and in a famous passage he tells us that faith, like other spiritual gifts, is empty and profitless if love is absent. The Reformers speak in a similar tone, as for example in the Anglican Homily of Salvation, where faith is defined as 'a sure trust and confidence in God's merciful promises to be saved from everlasting damnation by Christ; whereof doth follow a loving heart to obey His commandments'. Yet on the other hand it may be argued that to link two things together, however closely, is at the same time to treat them as distinct. By saying that love accompanies true faith, St. Paul implies that it is not actually a part of what he means by faith. It is a fact that he never says that love is a ground of justification; faith is so, and love is an inseparable concomitant of justifying faith and a sure test of its presence. This is the Reformation doctrine too. And so the suggestion that Pauline faith includes love as part of its meaning must be rejected as an oversimplification.

A precise and definitive analysis of Pauline 'faith' is hard to

[1] Catholic theology does not use the word *fides* in the sense of Pauline *pistis* at all, but of course that does not mean that Catholics know nothing of *pistis* in real life. They give it another name and discuss it in a different context. There is an excellent Catholic account of Abrahamic faith under another name in de Caussade's *Self-Abandonment to Divine Providence*.

come by, but perhaps we can see in what direction it must lie. I have already argued that 'faith' can justify only if and as it is not merely a belief, not even a specially confident belief, but a spring of action, and the New Testament certainly appears to speak of it as such. But must we rush to assume that there can be no spring of action other than hope or love in the Pauline sense of these words? The question, once fairly put, surely answers itself. Human nature is more complex, and the operations of grace in it are more various, than that. What we need to complete our conception of faith is what I have variously referred to as 'self-commitment', 'self-surrender', or simply 'responsiveness'. No doubt this will always be present where love is, but the essential nature of it and the essential nature of love are not the same.

This is probably as far as we ought to go in an exposition of St. Paul. He was no formal psychologist, and if we try to carry analysis much further than this we shall enter regions where he never ventured. Let us leave that to theological and psychological specialists, and turn our attention to another aspect of the problem of saving faith – the problem of its relation to the sacraments and especially to baptism.

I began this lecture with a quotation from St. Paul in which salvation, faith and baptism were linked together. I have discussed what is meant by 'faith' in this connection, and what part faith plays in our salvation. The part played by baptism remains to be explored. The question opens out into a wider one, that of the nature and function of all the sacraments. For all sacraments bear some relation to our life in Christ, they all in some sense bring Christ effectively to us; but Christians are not agreed as to how they do this, or how far their action may be dependent on the presence of faith in the recipient.

There is a type of theology which might almost be said to preach salvation by the sacraments, for it sees them as the principal channels through which, in the Christian economy, grace is imparted. Baptism sows the seed of new life in the soul, confirmation brings it to maturity, Holy Communion nourishes it, and so on through the whole list of the sacraments. One could use their names as the framework for a treatise on the spiritual life; for there is no stage in the development of that life which is not expressed in the symbolism of the sacraments and supported by their efficacy. That efficacy (it is emphasised) is not a product of, nor at all commensurate with the good dispositions of the celebrant or the recipient. It springs from Christ's own legislative will, and is inherent in the sacraments themselves by virtue of His will; nor can our dispositions add anything to the inherent power of the sacraments, though they may oppose a barrier (*obex*) to our reception of the benefit intended, and may hasten or delay the working out of its consequences in our minds and wills. This type of doctrine accordingly sees no problem in the baptism of infants, who cannot receive the sacrament with conscious faith and devotion. The essential effect of the sacrament does not depend on such conscious dispositions, and while of course an infant is incapable of expressing its union with Christ in terms of a mature Christian character, it is also incapable of raising a barrier of ill will against the gift of that union in such form as is appropriate to a child.

Such is the Catholic doctrine of the sacraments, and it has one obvious and great advantage. It treats the sacraments unmistakably as works of God and not of men. That should recommend it to the Protestants, who are so concerned to cast down human pride and to emphasise the sovereignty of God as the only Giver of gifts. Unhappily they have not been able to see it in that light, because it seems to threaten their other great principle of justification by faith alone. If baptism by the mere virtue of the sacrament washes out the stain of original sin and unites the soul with Christ, that is as much as to say that it imparts justification, and if it does this for infants who are incapable of performing an act of faith, we may well ask how justification can be said to depend on faith. Rather than allow this principle to be put in doubt or qualified in any way, classical Protestant theology has chosen to rewrite the doctrine of the sacraments in such a way as to make them clearly ancillary to faith.

A strong current of Reformation theology maintains that the sacraments are to be regarded as 'signs' and 'seals' of the promises of God. The conception is Pauline; for in Romans 4.11 we read how Abraham was given circumcision as a 'sign' and 'seal' of his justification. Accordingly Calvin defines a sacrament as 'an outward sign by which our Lord shows and testifies to us His good will towards us, in order to sustain and strengthen the weakness of our faith'. Similarly the Heidelberg Catechism defines the sacraments as 'visible, holy signs and seals which God has instituted in order by their means to convey the promise of the gospel with special clarity to us', and it goes on to say 'the Holy Ghost teaches in the gospel and confirms through the holy sacraments'. But the seal on a document is of no use to anyone unless he has read the document and is interested in its contents and so by analogy we may argue that the sacraments, as seals of the divine promises, are of no use to anyone who has not already encountered the promises and understood and embraced them – in short, to anyone who does not approach the sacraments in faith. In this spirit the Augsburg Confession says that the sacraments 'require faith, and are then rightly used when we receive them in faith and strengthen our faith thereby'. Scripture itself may be thought to present baptism in the same light when it couples it with faith and puts faith first: 'He who believes and is baptised shall be saved, and he who does not believe shall be condemned.' Being baptised seems to be presented here as a natural consequence of believing, but it is the faith, not the baptism, which is salvific. Baptism, in short, does not of itself initiate the soul's life in Christ, but strengthens it when it has been initiated by faith.

The Anglican Article 27 appears to take the same view when

it says that in baptism 'the promises of the forgiveness of sin and of our adoption ... are visibly signed and sealed, faith is confirmed and grace increased'. Faith cannot be confirmed nor grace increased when faith does not yet exist and grace has not yet been bestowed. The Article seems therefore to be saying that the characteristic operation of baptism is upon those who already have faith and are in a state of grace. But I will not dwell further upon that bewildering Article. Rather I will point to the straightforward and uncompromising expression of this theology in the teaching and practice of the Baptists. It is the one and only distinguishing principle of the Baptist connection that baptism is meant for those who have faith and should never be administered to those who have not, i.e. to infants. The only true and proper baptism is believers' baptism.

This might well seem to be the only consistent conclusion from the doctrine of baptism as the seal of a promise, yet we all know that the great majority of Protestants at all times, while conceiving baptism as a seal, have continued to baptise infants. What justification can there be for this? There is a very simple one. It is not in fact always necessary for a promise to be intelligible to its beneficiary at the time when it is made. One may quite well say of a child at birth that if, when he is grown up, he fulfils certain conditions, he may count on the reception of certain benefits and one may seal this promise in whatever way is judged appropriate, in order that as the child comes to years of understanding he may find the promise and the seal of it already in existence. There is no difficulty in interpreting baptism in this way. The child, by being baptised, is not made actually a member of Christ – only faith could make him that – but he has received God's promise, signed with God's seal, that if and when in later life he does believe he shall indeed be a member of Christ, and justified. The existence of this promise, so sealed, may actually prove powerful in awakening faith when the time comes, and the religious education of the child should attempt to use it in this way. The child should be told what God has promised and invited to comply with the conditions of the promise. It is thus that Calvin explains and defends infant baptism. The promise contained in baptism is profitless, he says, to one who has no faith, but still in itself it is a true and firm promise. As we grow up we are taught its meaning, and when we come to have a lively faith, we embrace the promise and have the full benefit of it. Similar teaching is implicit in Luther's *Greater Catechism*.

This conception of baptism is simple and plausible, and can appeal to certain elements in scripture, but it is not the traditional doctrine of the Church. The traditional doctrine, both Orthodox and Catholic, is that baptism actually regenerates, even when administered to infants. And since, of course, regeneration must include justification, and since infants are incapable of acts of faith, it seems to follow that justification can be had in the absence of faith. It is interesting to observe how this traditional view survives in the Reformers, in defiance of the logic of their overt principles. They could not so easily cast off the Catholicism in which they had been brought up. Thus the Anglican rite of baptism asserts that the child which has been baptised has been regenerated, made God's child by adoption, and incorporated into God's holy Church. In an Anglican document this is perhaps not very surprising. But Calvin too in a striking passage appeals to Scripture, to the examples of John the Baptist and of our Lord Himself, to show that it is possible for a child to be sanctified 'from his mother's womb'. To the question, how this is possible, he replies that the work of God, though beyond the reach of our understanding is not therefore null, and that the regeneration of infants is as 'possible and easy for Him' as it is 'secret and hidden from us.'

These are striking admissions, coming from such a source. How can they be reconciled with the view that faith is universally necessary to justification? Shall we say that a child, having now no faith, is justified through God's prevision of the faith he will one day come to have? This is just the kind of convenient fiction which I have tried to expel from other parts of the doctrine of the Atonement. Shall we say that the child is justified by the faith of the Church and more particularly of his sponsors? That the prayers of the Church work mightily is of course undeniable, but that they can take the place of faith in a person who has none is surely another convenient fiction. If the child is to be justified by faith, it must be neither someone else's faith nor the faith which he himself is to have when he is grown up, but a faith which he somehow has here and now in his infancy. Yet what could we mean by ascribing 'faith' to an infant? For it is agreed that the infant cannot perform those functions of mind and will which constitute the normal meaning of the word 'faith'. The only meaning which I can give to the phrase is that the child somehow receives in and through baptism what in scholastic Latin would be called a *habitus* of faith, i.e. an aptitude to perform acts of faith as soon as his age and his knowledge allow. Such an aptitude is not full-blown faith, but it is not nothing, and it 'has the nature' of faith. In this way and only in this way can the doctrine of baptismal regeneration and the doctrine of justification by faith alone be combined.

Be it confessed that this is something of a strain, yet this is not the only readjustment that we shall have to make. Justification must also mean something less for a child than for a mature person. Not that God's good will is any less toward the child, but the child is in important respects less able to know it and respond to it. In a being which is incapable of reflection and deliberate choice, neither sin nor the forgiveness of sin can be what we usually understand by those terms. No doubt a child after baptism is more closely united with God than before; he is a member of Christ and receives such gifts of grace as a child is capable of receiving; nor need this fact be quite as unintelligible to us as it seems to have been to Calvin. But while on the one hand some elements of estrangement are absent from the child's life, since he has no actual sin, on the other hand some features of atonement are also missing, since there is no knowledge of God and no deliberate turning to Him. What is 'reconciliation' when one of the parties was never consciously estranged and knows nothing of the ending of the estrangement? What is 'forgiveness' when the forgiven party knows nothing of it or of the need for it?

The truth is that both justification and faith in the Pauline sense belong to adults, and St. Paul was not thinking of children at all when he wrote. He hardly needed to. The great bulk of his converts were adults, for whom the problems which we are now discussing did not arise. They heard the preaching of the Word, they received the gift of faith, they made public profession of their faith, they were baptised and confirmed, in that order of time. Their baptism therefore was a believers' baptism in the modern Protestant sense; the baptism of an adult always is so. Child baptisms, if any took place at all in apostolic times, must have been very few in comparison with those of adults, and in fact it was several centuries before infant baptism became the rule in the Church. Only then did it become necessary to analyse and distinguish the respective functions of faith and of the baptismal rite; only when justification by faith is treated as an absolute and inviolable principle, a touchstone for all other teaching, does the problem become acute.

The conclusion to which I am led is that the doctrine of justification by faith must not be treated in that way. It was never meant as a piece of scientific analysis, a contribution towards a systematic theology. It is an attempt, and a brilliantly successful one, to lay bare the central nerve of the Old Testament, the central principle of God's dealings with Israel and with all mankind; it is written in a strongly polemical spirit. The dialectical edge of the phrase 'by faith' lies in its negative implication, 'not by works'. The heart of the meaning is that our deliverance from the consequences of sin and from sin itself is God's work and not our own, a gift to us and not our achievement. God alone is the Saviour, and to Him alone glory is due; from the beginning to the end man is dependent upon Him. In an adult human being who has been properly instructed, that dependence should be conscious and should take the form of Abrahamic faith, and it is an important moment in a man's growth towards spiritual maturity when he awakens to the significance of the Epistle to the Romans. Protestant tradition is fully justified in emphasising this as it does. But this is merely one stage, and not the first stage, in the normal path of the soul's development under favourable conditions. It is not an absolute and inflexible requirement before a man can become a member of Christ. God bestows grace where He will; He has declared His will to bestow it in the sacraments. It has long seemed to me, and I think history confirms it, that the Reformation principle of the sovereign grace of God is set forth and embodied in Catholic teaching and practice not less truly, and a good deal less abstractly, than in the Reformation doctrines themselves.

Index